M000291295

THE

LESS THAN PERFECT CHILD

A Journey From The Trenches Of Dysfunctionality
To Life As A Surgeon

Dr. David C. Bardsley

Published by Silver Eagle Media
PO 4153 Aspen, CO 81612

thelessthanperfectchild.com

THE LESS THAN PERFECT CHILD. by Dr. David Bardsley

First printing 2011

Published by

Silver Eagle Media, PO 4153, Aspen, CO 81612

For information thelessthanperfectchild.com

Library of Congress Catalogue Number

20119909697

David Collins Bardsley

The less than perfect child / David C. Bardsley

ISBN 978-0-9835446-0-9

1. Inspiration 2. Psychology 3. Parenting

Cover Design – www.cidcreative.com

Interior design – www.nu-imagedesign.com

To all those destined to live life as a ***less than perfect child*** and to the parents who love them.

CONTENTS

PROLOGUE

Growing up with a behavioral or learning disability is never easy; not for the parents, not for the teachers, and especially not for the affected child. Although some of the problems diminish or disappear by adolescence, others remain for a lifetime.

The past two decades have seen an unprecedented explosion in the diagnosis of Asperger's, Tourette's, ADHD, autism, OCD, and other behavioral and learning disabilities. One in 10 male children takes a psychostimulant, such as Ritalin and Adderall; one in 110 is on the autistic spectrum; and 200,000 suffer with Tourette's. Many of those affected are now in their late teens and early adulthood. What will their future be?

Knowing you are *different* and unable to do anything about it can produce a psychological scar that lasts a lifetime. Although many books on the subject have been written by clinical experts and struggling parents, few have been written by an afflicted individual.

I wrote this book to give hope to the millions of troubled parents who worry about what the future holds for their "less than perfect child" and to help the countless adults who have never been diagnosed, yet struggle daily with these disorders.

CHAPTER ONE
"A GOOD BOY IS A TIRED BOY"

"Get out! Get out of my classroom, right now!"

Usually, I tried to make myself invisible by hiding at the back of the class; only the smart kids sat up front. But I couldn't hide from Mr. Whalen's angry words. Everyone in that room knew they were meant for me. For the first time in my life, I felt the pain of humiliation and shame. I was six years old.

By the time I entered first grade, I had developed into a bizarre little boy, adopting a number of peculiar and apparently annoying behaviors, not the least of which were my vocalizations. I made strange nnnnnnoises when I spoke. The letter 'n' was my nemesis; I somehow felt it was necessary to blurt it out and then drag out the sound as long as I could.

"David, would you like another slice of pie?"

"N-n-n-n-no, thank you, but I would like a-n-n-n-n-nother glass of milk."

I had also developed uncontrollable facial tics, blinking, grimaces, and spastic head jerks. *Rain Man* had nothing on me. And if that weren't bizarre enough; I had become a spinner. For whatever reason, I was compelled to take three steps in one direction, spin in a circle, then take another three steps and spin in the opposite direction. On and on it went. It took me forever to get anywhere.

There were no school lunches or cafeterias in those days so everyone went home at noon. My brother walked home in fifteen minutes; it took me thirty, which meant I only had four or five minutes to eat lunch before it was time to start spinning my way back to school.

"Why are you doing that?" was a constant question.

"I don't kn-n-n-n-now; I just have to."

My young parents, Bob and Irene, became understandably worried and frightened. The first stop was the family physician. After a long series of tests and evaluations, Dr. Donner finally told them, "I have no idea what's wrong with him. This is one strange little boy you have here. As a matter of fact, I have never seen anything quite like it."

That was the beginning of what became a very long journey. Over the next two-and-a-half years, I was poked, prodded, and percussed by no fewer than seven different specialists. The pediatrician diagnosed Saint Vitus Dance, which turned out to be incorrect.

"I think his nervous system is exhausted," the neurologist concluded. "He needs some rest, even if we have to force it upon him."

So there I was: a hyperactive eight-year-old in an adult institution, confined to complete bed rest. I was not physically strapped to the bed, but I was so doped up and sedated that I wasn't even capable of spinning to the bathroom and back.

My teacher, Miss Martinez, came to visit me two or three times and tried to help so I wouldn't fall behind in my school work. It was hopeless; I hardly knew where I was and could barely utter my own name. David didn't have my favorite letter *n* in it anyway, so where was the satisfaction?

For the first two weeks I had a roommate, Mr. Haley, who said he was a barber. I didn't believe him for a minute; he was old and feeble and his hands shook way too much. Along with his obvious mental problems he had some kind of surgical wound in his lower back that was badly infected. Every day at two o'clock sharp, Nurse Finley would barge into the room carrying a large tray of gauze bandages and bottles of foul-smelling maroon-colored liquids. No hello or greeting of any sort, just the same terse question, "You're not going to throw up today, are you?"

"N-n-n-n-o. Please, please, let me go out of the room while you do that, please."

"You know the rules; you're not allowed out of bed."

The moment she began removing the dressing from Mr. Haley's wound a foul, purulent stench would fill the room, and my projectile vomit would follow. Despite holding the kidney basin close to my chin, most of my stomach contents would end up on the bed sheets and the floor. Nurse Finley would berate me as she changed Mr. Haley's dressing. I was terrified of Nurse Finley. Moments after she left the room, a small stooped Asian woman, who never spoke, would appear with a mop and bucket. I was allowed to sit on the chair beside the bed while she cleaned the floor and changed the sheets.

This horrible routine continued every day, for two weeks, until Mr. Haley was taken away. I repeatedly asked if he had died but my question always went unanswered. After all, I was a less than perfect child.

Eventually I was released from the hospital so the doctors could determine how much improvement all this tranquilized rest had brought me. I had improved all right; after two or three days, the effects of the medications had worn off and I was able to spin faster than ever.

The final stop on that long journey was a child psychiatrist, Dr. Woodward. I had to wait nine months just to get an appointment with him, and after that the weekly visits lasted for another six months. I disliked him from the beginning. He was cold, never smiled, always stared at me, and then scribbled something on a notepad. He asked stupid questions like: "David, do the girls in your class make you feel any different than the boys in your class?"

"What do you mean-n-n-n?"

"Well, do you feel differently when you talk to girls compared to when you talk to boys?"

I was certain he could feel my embarrassment but I held my ground, "N-n-n-no."

"Not ever?"

"N-n-n-never."

"Ok, let's play some hockey."

He'd go to the closet, remove a table-top hockey game, and place it on his desk. Long before the advent of video games, most boys had a hockey game that somewhat resembled a foosball table, but without the legs. My brothers and I played for hours on end. The players were controlled by long rods that slide in and out to make them move along the playing surface. I can only assume that Dr. Woodward thought the game provided a distraction as he pumped a stream of questions at me. I found the whole exercise utterly boring. In the six months of weekly visits I never failed to score less than twenty goals per session. He never scored once. His players were constantly offside but I never bothered to tell him.

The day of the last visit finally arrived and I will never forget my parent's excitement. I'm sure they thought he was going to tell them there was some simple treatment, pill, or medication I could be given to be normal.

We arrived early for the appointment that day, but as usual we were kept waiting about an hour. The reception area was stark; the drab grey walls were bare and there was no music, just awkward silence. We waited on chrome chairs covered in floral-pattern cushions and cold transparent plastic.

Dr. Woodward eventually came out of his office, shuffled down a long corridor, and met us at the reception desk. Barely acknowledging me, he nodded his head towards my parents and then, without saying a word, led the three of us toward his office. A feeling of dread overcame me. *Was he jealous of me? Should I have let him win at least one game?* When we got to his office doorway, he stopped and pointed to a small wooden chair beside the door. "David, I want you to wait here." He then led my parents into his office and closed the door, but not all the way. It remained open an inch or so, just enough for me to hear every word.

"Well, as you know, I've had six months to evaluate your son and the first thing I want you to understand is that, it's not your fault. It's not anything you have done or anything you haven't done, and it's certainly not his fault. However, David is going to need a great deal of special care and attention. The first thing I am going to recommend is that you immediately take him out of school so we can put him in a special training program where he will have the opportunity to learn some valuable life skills. I am telling you this because he will never progress past the sixth grade."

Then came the words that haunt me to this day: "Look, there is no easy way to tell you this; your son is mentally retarded."

I was stunned. After a brief silence I heard my father yelling. My father never yelled. He seldom even raised his voice. A few seconds later, I heard the psychiatrist yelling and then my mother joined in. As I jumped off the chair to see what all the commotion was about, the receptionist rushed by, pushed me aside, and knocked me to the floor. She burst through the office doors while I got up as quickly as I could, spun around (I was good at that) and raced into the office. I felt amused and confused by what I saw.

My father, the mildest mannered person you could ever possibly meet, lost it—big time. I guess all those years of hope, frustration, and emotion boiled over when he heard that diagnosis of *mentally retarded* and he came unglued. He grabbed Dr. Woodward by his tie, dragged him across the desk, and tried to punch him but my mother was hanging from my father's cocked arm. The receptionist jumped on my father's back, wrapped her legs around his waist, and put him into a chokehold. Their bodies were so entangled they looked like octopuses in some sort of mating ritual. It was absolute pandemonium, and there in the door-way stood the retarded nine-year-old, staring in disbelief. *Was it my fault?*

A few minutes later my father calmed down and I will never forget the look on his face when he turned and saw me standing in the doorway. He rushed over, took me by the hand, and said, "David, you're *not* retarded." He spun around and pointed to Dr. Woodward. "He is!"

We stormed out of the office and on the way to the car my father stopped, knelt down on one knee, and said, "There is nothing wrong with you, David. You just have too much energy. The only good boy is a tired boy, so from now on your job is to stay outside and play as much as you can. I want you to tire yourself out." Saying that to a hyperactive child is like telling someone with a sweet tooth their job is to eat as much candy as they can. I was in heaven.

My parents were not sure what to do after that. There was no network of social agencies to turn to for help, so they took matters into their own hands. They listened to their gut feelings and had the courage to follow them. They understood that the intellect is easily fooled but the heart never is.

From that day on they promised, "No more doctors, no more therapists, no more hospitals, no special schools or therapy of any kind."

My parents replaced the drugs, the treatments, and the diagnosis with their unyielding support, their relentless encouragement, and their love; their uncompromising love.

School, however, did not get any easier. As a matter of fact, things got worse. My verbal outbursts occurred frequently. The letter 'n' was ruining my life. I hated the letter 'n'. I hate it still to this day. I was constantly reminded of just how different I was.

"Hey, Blinkey."

"Here comes Twitcher."

"Retard."

There were lots of nicknames. Kids can be cruel. I know my father had some idea of what I was going through, because he bought me a set of boxing gloves. Against my mother's wishes, he taught my brother and me how to use them, and he taught us well. We weren't supposed to fight inside the house but on those long, cold winter days, my brother and I would push back the furniture in the living room, lace on the gloves, and start wailing away on each other. Every table and shelf in that living room was filled with small porcelain figurines. Collecting them was my mother's passion. Invariably, we would break one. My mother would hear the crash and run to the living room in a fury

"You just wait! Wait until your father gets home! You are in such big trouble, mister."

When my father came home from work, he would storm into the living room and stand there with clenched fists and an angry look on his face and shout in a voice loud enough for my mother to hear, "How many times have I told you kids not to fight inside the house?"

Then he would glance over his shoulder to make sure my mother wasn't watching and whisper to us, "Now remember, two jabs are always followed by an uppercut—jab-jab-uppercut, protect your chin. Now let's see you do it." Then he would yell again for my mother to hear. "If I catch you fighting inside again I am going to tan your hides."

When the teasing and the bullying became too much to bear, those lessons I learned in that living room served me well in the school yards and playgrounds of my life. We're taught that it's always best to turn the other cheek but sometimes, just sometimes, you have to stand your ground, even if you are nine years old.

My parents never acted upset when I came home with a black eye or bloody nose; they seemed to expect it. My father always asked the same two questions, "Who started it?" and "Did it end well?"

Bullying and teasing will always be part of childhood. Those with physical disabilities are often made fun of but seldom to their face. Not so for children who look normal but behave "differently." They are the easiest targets and persecuted relentlessly.

Parents can't be with their children twenty-four hours a day. There will always be some circumstances you can't protect them from. All you can do is give them the tools and trust they will use them wisely. Self-confidence and self-esteem are the cornerstones for the development of any less than perfect child.

CHAPTER TWO
"THE LESS THAN PERFECT CHILD"

My father was the youngest of seven children. His father died when he was fifteen and six months later his mother died. He said it was from a broken heart. He worked for several years in the family's small hat-making business to save enough money for college but WWII had other plans for him. He and his brother Jack joined the Air Force, and he spent the next four years flying submarine patrol out of the Shetland Islands, off the northern tip of Scotland. My mother waited for his safe return.

Shortly after the war ended he married my mother, and soon after my brother Michael, the first of the Baby Boomers arrived, and all hopes of a university education ended. It was one of the great regrets of my father's life and the reason he regarded education above all else. Whenever we drove past workers toiling in a ditch beside the road or doing heavy labor, he would say, "See those men, David? They didn't study their lessons."

Despite all the encouragement and support, I was never able to forget that I was different. People stared, looking away quickly when I caught them. That was followed by the dreaded whispers, "*What's wrong with him?*" If I only knew.

One of the biggest fears I had was reading out loud in class. I would stammer and fumble over the simplest of words. My classmates would turn and stare at me. My twitching and head jerks worsened and n-n-n-noises became even harder to control. The laughter and snickering were unbearable. I quickly learned to adapt.

Reading would start at the front of the row and each student in turn would stand up at their desk and read a paragraph or two. When one row was complete, the front of the next row would start. The classes were large, 28 to 30 students each. I would sit in the very last seat in one of the middle rows and when the first person in my row started reading, I would wait until the teacher was not looking, then slide over to the last seat in the row that had just finished reading. I was rarely caught, but my reading skills would be an embarrassment all my life.

My parents recognized my deficiency long before the teachers. They bought a home reading improvement course and spent countless hours helping me. Progress was painfully slow, but things did improve. Decades would pass before I learned that this lack of fluency in reading aloud is a frequent sign of dyslexia, but the condition was virtually unknown at the time.

* * *

"Damn you, get away from me! Move that fucking car. Move that fucking car."

It was a hot summer day in my eleventh year. We were in the middle of town stopped at a red light; windows down, the crosswalk in front of us empty. On the sidewalk waiting to cross stood the Umbrella Lady. Although probably only in her fifties, her frail body and weather-beaten face made her look more like a 70 -year-old. Her thin body arched backward and her left arm rose awkwardly above her head, grasping the handle of a closed umbrella. She walked the streets of downtown every day, rain or shine, in a long, dirty raincoat, holding the closed umbrella over her head, cursing at people who did not exist. As children we were afraid of her, crossing to the other side of the street whenever we saw her approaching.

"Don't stare," my father said. "It's not her fault; she's retarded."

Although two years had passed, it was impossible for me to erase the memory of the psychiatrist telling my parents I was retarded. For many months after the Umbrella Lady incident, I could not help thinking, *Am I like that? Is that what people think of me—retarded?*

I fared much better outside of school. Large for my age, the years of hyperactivity served me well. It was simply play for the sake of movement that brought me the most joy. I ran, jumped, climbed, swung, threw, swam, crawled, skipped, and spun until I was exhausted and loved every minute of it. Because of this, my strength, speed, balance, coordination, and timing were far more advanced than my peers. This gave me a great advantage later in life when it came to organized sports. I excelled, and this greatly helped me gain confidence, and acceptance by others, despite my obvious differences. My parents never understood why, but they realized early on that all my peculiar symptoms decreased when I was physically tired. So they always encouraged activity, whatever it was.

I loved climbing trees. Maples were my favorite. Their large, smooth branches were not full of annoying little twigs that impeded climbing, like the barbs on spruce and firs. One afternoon, I was racing my only friend Buddy to the top of our favorite tree, a huge maple, in a field near our home. Buddy was two branches above me and I did not want to lose the race. I squatted low and leapt with all my strength, arms outstretched like Superman toward the branch Buddy was standing on. Unlike Superman, I fell short of my intended target. I grappled onto a much smaller branch underneath. I was dangling precariously when Buddy yelled, "Watch out! It's breaking!"

The branch snapped off and when I hit the ground I was knocked unconscious. Buddy ran to get my father, and they quickly returned in the car. I was sitting up, half stunned, when they arrived.

There was a terrible pain in my right arm which was bent at an awkward angle. I was sure it was broken but my father said, "No David, it doesn't look too bad; just a little crooked. Here let me straighten it a bit."

Despite my shrill scream, he assured me it was probably just a sprain. "No, Dad, I think it's broken. It hurts a lot, and look, I can't move my fingers."

After much arguing and at my insistence, we finally drove to the hospital. The x-rays confirmed that my arm was indeed broken, in two locations, and my arm was put in a cast. On the drive home, I was mesmerized by my swollen, discolored fingers protruding from the end of my shiny white cast.

My father stopped the car and reached over to open my door. After I hopped out and closed the door he said, "Make sure you are home by dark," and sped off.

It took me several moments to realize I was not home. He had driven me back to the same tree. For a brief moment, I felt betrayed. Then I saw Buddy and Will running along the edge of the field. I bent down, picked up a stick, and started chasing after them. I guess my father was following his belief: *"The only good boy is a tired boy."*

* * *

My family accepted my strangeness and I always felt safe around them. I had two brothers: Michael, eighteen months older, and Peter, five years younger. My mother's father died when she was sixteen, so the only grandparent I ever knew was my maternal grandmother. She moved in with my parents the day they returned from their honeymoon. It was like having two mothers under one roof. At times, it seemed like they were competing to see who the best homemaker was. Because of this, there were rarely any chores for me to do. My job was to tire myself out.

Saturday was hockey night in Canada. The entire nation would sit around their televisions to watch their favorite team. There were only six to choose from back then. My grandmother was a great hockey fan and her team was the Montreal Canadians. On the floor above lived our wonderful neighbors, Don and Jessie, transplants from Toronto. Whenever Montreal scored, my grandmother would take a broom and bang the handle on the ceiling and yell, "*Losers.*" When Toronto scored, Don would stomp on the floor and she would be furious.

In those days, black and white TVs had horizontal and vertical holds which could be adjusted manually. At the start of each period my grandmother would fiddle with both controls simultaneously, until the picture was slightly horizontally tipped toward the Toronto goal. She thought somehow this helped her beloved Canadians skate downhill. She would reverse the process when the teams changed ends at the beginning of each period. She could not accept Montreal losing, but she accepted me the way I was.

***

"What's wrong?" asked my classmate Bill.

We were in gross anatomy lab and had just finished unwrapping the new cadaver assigned to us. I was staring in stunned silence thinking how much it resembled my grandmother when the instructor interrupted and said I had a phone call in the office.

"Get here as quick as you can" my father told me. "Your grandmother has had a massive heart attack; it doesn't look good."

Five hours later I entered the hospital room just as they were pulling the sheet over her head. For the twenty-six years I knew her, she never once mentioned my strangeness, asked what was wrong with me, or tried to explain my bizarre behavior to others. I loved her.

My Little Secret

"Hey Dave, you want to come over to my house tonight? Rickey and Billy are coming over. My dad just flooded the rink in the backyard and put some lights on it. We can play hockey as late as we want and my mom said we could all sleep in the basement."

"Gee, Tommy, I'd love to but I have to do some stuff with my family tonight. Call me tomorrow if you are going to play."

Sadness and shame swept over me as I hung up the phone. There was no place I would have rather been than playing hockey with my friends in Tommy's backyard and sleeping over in the basement. Hockey was my passion, and I was the best in the neighborhood. Everyone knew it. Instead of being shunned, everyone wanted me on their team. For the first time in my life I was recognized as being special in a good way, and I loved it.

There was no family function I had to attend that evening. I had lied to Tommy, just like I lied to every other friend who asked me to spend the night at their house. I was harboring a dark secret and I was terrified someone would find out.

I was eleven years old and I still wet the bed.

My brothers rarely teased me about it. I am sure my father put the fear of God in them if they ever did. The doctor said there was nothing wrong with me physically, and I would likely grow out of it. My parents tried fluid restriction and all the usual things but nothing worked.

I would lay awake at night as long as I could trying not to fall asleep, worrying and hoping that it would not happen again. Occasionally I would awaken to the delight of dry sheets, and I would be euphoric, certain that I had "licked it." My joy, however, was short lived as the following night the old habit would return with a vengeance.

When the family went on vacations my mother always brought a special rubber sheet and extra cotton ones. My parents were never angry nor scolded me about my problem. Despite their constant reassurances that I would "grow out of it," I lived in constant fear that my brothers would tell their friends or my parents would discuss my problem with other parents and eventually the other kids would find out. It never happened.

As an adult looking back, the problem seems trivial, almost humorous. For a child living through it, it is monumental. I was peculiar enough already and I didn't need another special trait to further set me apart. I was forever grateful to my family for keeping my secret. Children need many things, but most of all they need to know they can completely trust the people who love them. Telling them is not enough; they need to be shown. Years later, I would discover that prolonged bedwetting is a very common problem in children with Attention Deficit Hyperactivity Disorder, or ADHD.

The Mohawk

"How do you want it cut?

"I would like a flat top please, but not too short."

It was two o'clock on a Saturday afternoon late in October. It was overcoat cold outside, but I was seated in the window chair of Marr's Barber Shop, and the sun was streaming through the glass making the whole setting nearly tropical. Normally Mr. Marr cut my hair, but he had three clients waiting so I went with Mr. Hall. His thin grey hair, grey eyebrows, grey mustache, and wrinkled grey skin (that was completely yellow on his chain smoking hand) made his worn barbers' tunic seem all the whiter. He looked a hundred years old although I am sure he was much younger.

Normally, I would have waited for Mr. Marr, but I was in a hurry to meet the gang and some new girls at Toni's Restaurant that night. What worried me most about Mr. Hall was the pronounced tremor he had in both hands. Strangely, it disappeared almost completely when he came at your head with the clippers. But I was still apprehensive.

Barbers seldom used scissors in those days. The hypnotic buzz of the electric clippers combined with the sun streaming through the window, warming the entire right side of my body, made me sleepy, and I nearly nodded off several times. I fought it but it finally happened.

As I lost consciousness my head slowly lowered forward until my chin rested firmly on my chest. As it did Mr. Hall followed it peacefully down, all the while cutting with his electric clippers. Then, as it often happens to me when I fall asleep in a chair, my head reflexively jerked to an upright position. Mr. Hall had no time to react and the result was a six-inch long, two inch wide bald strip, right down the middle of my head—a reverse Mohawk.

Mr. Hall was very apologetic, even though it was entirely my fault. He offered to shave the rest of my head, but I declined. So the reverse Mohawk stayed. I made jokes about it inside the barber shop but what was left of my self-confidence disappeared the minute I stepped into the street. I tried to convince myself that it might be a good thing, distracting others from noticing my twitching and head jerking as much.

I did not go to Toni's restaurant that evening. I did not leave the house for two days. But Monday morning arrived all too soon and school awaited, where a strict *"No Hat"* policy was in place. I pleaded with my parents to let me stay home. They sympathized with my plight and made suggestions on how to deal with the impending ridicule. I decided humor was my best chance. I explained to the kids at school that it was a cool reverse Mohawk and I was from the famous Twitching Tribe. I did not start a trend. The staring and snickering were worse than ever.

Hell's Bells

"As I told you on the phone, Mrs. Bardsley, the altar boy training course is very intensive. It's only four months in duration and we've just completed the second month. It's half over. There will be another one next year."

"Please Mrs. MacDonald; my son David is quite special. I can assure you he will make up the missed sessions quickly. We will give him all the help he needs at home so he can finish the course with the other boys. Just give him a chance; you'll be proud of him. Please!"

So my formal training as an altar boy in the Catholic Church began. I have no idea why my mother was so intent on me becoming one. Perhaps she thought if I served God he would reciprocate by making me normal. My family was not particularly religious. We attended mass every Sunday and ate fish on Fridays, but God was rarely discussed at home.

I had personally harbored considerable resentment against the Catholic Church from the time I started school. The Archdiocese built two elementary schools—one Catholic, one Protestant—that were joined by a common gym. The local school board leased the complex from the Archdiocese with the agreement that the Catholic school would only have Catholic teachers and catechism would be taught at the end of each day. This meant the Protestant kids got out of school an hour earlier. This seemed grossly unfair. It seemed like God favored the Protestants.

On Sundays, most Catholic churches celebrated an hour long High Mass which included hymns, prayer, gospel readings, homily, and bells. Two altar boys were assigned to serve at each mass while ten to twelve fully robed alternates sat in pews facing the altar. The server on the right was assigned the responsibility of ringing the bells. Five or six hand bells are welded together on a metal frame with a large handle on top. At the appropriate time, the bells were rung, signaling the congregation to stand up, sit down, or kneel.

The training on proper bell use occurred during the first two months of altar boy training. I missed it completely.

One mass was offered weekday mornings. It was an abbreviated twenty minute version of the High Mass, devoid of singing, preaching, and bells. Rarely was it attended by more than the same ten parishioners. I often wondered why. Were they there to ask for something special from God, or were they just lonely and had no other place to go?

An altar boy had to serve eighteen to twenty weekday masses, a sort of apprenticeship, before being allowed to serve High Mass on Sunday. The head altar "boy," Paul, who knew as much about mass as any of the priests and was as old as them, made up the schedule, which was posted every Sunday in the vestry, the room where the altar boys robed.

One particular Sunday I was in a hurry to leave after mass and neglected to read the schedule for the upcoming week. The following Sunday I arrived just minutes before mass was to begin. The other altar boys had already taken their seats beside the altar and the vestry was empty except for Paul, who was steaming mad.

"You're late!" he screamed. "You know that servers have to be here fifteen minutes before mass starts. Father Donahue is furious."

"Server? I'm not the server today. Besides I've never done a high mass before."

"Didn't you read the schedule? You're on today. Come on! Let's go!"

He grabbed me by the arm and literally dragged me behind the altar to the priests' vestry on the opposite side, all the while dismissing my protests that I was not ready to serve High Mass.

Larry, the other server, was waiting for me beside the doorway leading to the altar. On a small wooden chair next to him sat Father Donahue, fully robed, eyes closed, head hung forward, sound asleep. Somewhere in his eighties, Father Donahue was the parish's oldest priest, and despite his two hearing aids, he was stone deaf.

He was also an altar boy's worst nightmare; everyone dreaded serving for him. He frequently became confused, skipped parts of the mass, and then came back to them inappropriately later on. You never knew where he was; *he* never knew where he was. They normally only allowed him to celebrate mass on low attendance week days, never on a Sunday.

A second priest, Father Graham, quickly entered the vestry and helped Father Donahue to his feet. He motioned to us and said, "Let's go!"

Larry followed Father Donahue. I stepped in line and tried to push Larry to the right, to the bell side, but he held his ground. A moment later the three of us were making our entrance onto the altar in front of the packed church. Father Graham took a seat with the other altar boys in the side pews.

In those days the altar was located at the very back of the raised platform in the front of the church. The priest stood facing the altar with his back to the congregation as he celebrated the mass. Things started reasonably well. Father Donahue only lost his place once or twice and Father Graham slipped out of his side pew and guided him back on track.

I was filled with dread knowing the time for the bells was near at hand. I knew the first sign for the ringing of the bells was when the priest faced the tabernacle (the ornate box where the unconsecrated Communion hosts are stored) and genuflected. But due to his advanced age Father Donahue's legs were very weak and they frequently buckled. So I had no way of knowing whether this was an attempt to genuflect or not. Finally, he turned his head around the best he could and looked at me. I took this as the signal for the bells and started ringing. Four hundred of the faithful immediately stood up.

His knees buckled again, deeper than before. Was this another attempt to genuflect, another signal? I started ringing again. Four hundred confused parishioners dropped to their knees.

I don't think Father Donahue even heard the bells. He made

another stiffened attempt to turn and look at me. *Was this another clue? What do I do?* My heart was pounding. I started ringing. Four hundred struggled to their feet. The bells continued. They stood, they knelt, they stood, and they knelt. They were as confused as me.

My raspberry face felt like it was about to explode and I twitched uncontrollably. My body was shaking so much the bells went off again. Half the congregation dutifully knelt while the other half simply sat down and waited in confusion. Father Graham rushed from his pew and grabbed the bells from my trembling hand.

"Do you have any idea what you are doing?" he uttered in a muffled rage. "Get off the altar. Now!"

He pointed to the vestry door and then motioned for one of the other alternates to take my place.

Humiliated and ashamed, I threw my robes on the vestry floor and ran home in tears. I hated the priest, the church, and then I took it out on God. "I hate you God."

My parents had been at the mass and witnessed my humiliation first hand. I told them I never wanted to go back. My father explained I should not quit if I really wanted to be an altar boy. I reminded them it was never my idea in the first place. They accepted my decision and did not pressure me to return.

Several weeks later I was attending Sunday mass with my parents. Father Graham recounted a remarkable story from the pulpit.

"Last weekend I was visiting a small orphanage in a very poor area. It was a miserably cold, rainy day. The buildings were arranged around a dirt courtyard that had completely turned to mud. I watched as a small boy tried to push a larger boy in a wheelchair through the mud and rain to the other side. The chair soon became bogged down, so the small boy lifted the larger boy out of the chair and struggled to carry him through the mud to the cafeteria. As they passed close by I called out, 'He must be very heavy'."

"'No Father, he ain't heavy; he's my brother.'"
There wasn't a dry eye in the church.

Three weeks later I was driving in the car with my family when a song by the Hollies came on the radio. The instant I heard the lyrics, "*He ain't heavy, he's my brother,*" I knew the priest had lied. He had heard the song and then made up the whole story. In my limited child's mind I had viewed priests as something uniquely special. They were perfect people, directed by God. How could a priest lie? I felt betrayed and confused. My parents explained that perhaps the boy had heard the song before the priest. I knew that was not true, he had lied. Perhaps God lies too.

CHAPTER THREE
"THE YELLOW MIST"

When World War II broke out, my father Bob and his brother Jack joined the Royal Canadian Air Force. Within a year they found themselves stationed in England on loan to the British Royal Air Force. Jack was in London and eventually piloted a Spitfire in the Battle of Britain. My father had the much more mundane task of flying a twin engine amphibious aircraft, a Catalina, on submarine patrol.

When he returned home from the war, my father wanted to start a flying club so he petitioned the city council in Saint John for a license. He was denied on the grounds a flying club already existed, and the councilors saw no need for two. The existing club was on an abandoned air strip and owned one plane, which had not been certified to fly for more than ten years, but it had a bar license and this was the reason the club still existed. My father gathered the evidence and made another presentation to city council. This time the new license was granted, the existing one revoked, and the new club grew quickly. Soon, a full-time manager and flight instructor were hired.

I became a hanger rat. Every weekend was spent at the club and whenever a plane rolled out for a lesson, I was in the back seat, my twitches and head jerks unseen and my vocalizations unheard. Despite the roar of the engine it was a place of wonderful isolation and peace. I felt safe. Sixteen was the legal age for a pilot's license and it seemed like an eternity away but I kept dreaming. By twelve I was a seasoned back seat pilot.

Eventually, a dispute erupted among the board members who wanted to turn the flying club into a for-profit business. This was never my father's intention. He resigned as chairman and never returned to the club.

Weeks later my father sat on the back porch enjoying a beer with his best friend Norm.

"You're going to *what*? Buy a sailboat? Bobby, you don't know how to sail."

"I can learn, Norm."

"Why in the world would you want to do such a thing?"

"It may keep my boys together a little longer."

Ed Mathews, a commercial pilot who regularly hung around the flying club, had spent three years sailing the world on a four-masted schooner. The tales he told would keep us spellbound for hours. He explained that sailing and flying had a great deal in common, and he convinced my father to buy a boat. He offered to teach us how to sail.

My older brother Michael and I had saved a total of two hundred dollars between us. My father said he would contribute four hundred dollars toward a sailboat. Our six-hundred-dollar budget eventually led us to Colonel Holder's boatyard and the *White Mist*."

The Colonel, a WWI veteran, had inherited the ramshackle old boatyard from his father. It was on a piece of land shaped like a ping pong paddle with a thin isthmus connecting it to the mainland; it was almost an island. The boatyard had no official employees; otherwise the department of safety would have shut it down immediately. There were about twenty boats, almost all wooden and in various stages of decay. The *White Mist* looked pretty derelict. She was twenty-two feet long and a two-berth cabin too small to stand up in. There was no engine, toilet, windows, or sink.

I loved her immediately.

The Colonel assured us she was basically a sound vessel and with some hard work she would be a fine yacht. A bill of sale was drawn up, the six hundred dollars handed over, and we were yacht owners.

Wooden boats dry out when not in the water and the seams between the planks open up. The Colonel showed us how to caulk the seams and prepare the bottom for the antifouling paint, which kept barnacles and worms from attaching to the wooden hull. Every weekend and evening that spring was spent caulking and sanding. It was tedious work but I loved it. The caulking paste was pushed into the gaping seams with the edge of a putty knife until it was overfilled. The excess was scraped off and allowed to dry before it was sanded smooth. My father and brother would fill three seams to my one; but mine was perfect. I obsessed over any minute irregularity and sanded meticulously until it blended perfectly into the adjacent wood.

"Dave, it doesn't have to be perfect; it will be under water," my father explained. "No one will see it."

I didn't care. I didn't know why but my seams had to be perfect.

Everyone was excited when we were finally ready for the paint. My father hopped in the car and disappeared into town. An hour later he returned to the boatyard with a gallon of special marine paint he found on sale for half price in a hardware store. That's how the *White Mist* became the *Yellow Mist*."

The boatyard was a magical place for a twelve-year-old. I loved every hour I spent there. The Colonel became a great friend and supporter. He was like the grandfather I never had. One evening I was helping move some barrels. My body was quiet as I rolled them to the end of the shed but I spun and twitched as I walked back to get the next one. One of the owners was staring at me as he sanded. I thought he disapproved of what I was doing.

"The Colonel asked me to move these barrels," I told him.

He just looked away; they always looked away. Later I heard him ask. "What's wrong with him?"

"*Nothing*," barked the Colonel. "He just has too much energy. You would be a lucky man if your lazy kids were more like him."

I loved the Colonel.

The big day for the launch finally came. The *Yellow Mist* had a four-foot deep keel so it sat in a wooden cradle which made the deck about seven feet off the ground. Six-inch diameter logs were placed in front of the cradle and acted as rollers as five or six people with long crowbars pried the boat forward and onto a rusted railway car. The wooden cradle was lashed to the car so it would not float away during the launching. A long rusted cable was attached to the railcar on one end and to a rusted winch on the other. I climbed up into the cockpit and held on. The brake was released and the car, cradle and boat headed down the rusty rails toward the water. The boat shook violently as it picked up speed, and I was frightened it would fall off the rails; then we hit the water.

As the car submerged beneath the surface, the *Yellow Mist* floated free. My heart swelled with pride. It was the most magnificent sight I had ever seen. Tim, a part-time yard helper was waiting nearby in a small skiff equipped with an outboard. With some urgency he threw me a tow line which I quickly attached to the bow cleat. He jerked the outboard into gear and started towing the *Yellow Mist* as fast as possible into the nearby cove. Despite all the calking we had jammed into the seams, water flooded into the hull at a frightening rate. We were sinking.

"Faster, Tim," I screamed. "Faster!"

It was no use. He was staring straight ahead at the approaching shore and couldn't hear me over the roar of the engine.

The *Yellow Mist* had almost sunk to the level of the deck when the keel finally hit bottom and we came to an abrupt halt.

"Throw the anchor down," Tim yelled. Then he came alongside, I got into the skiff and we headed for shore. A terrible sadness came over me as I looked back at the half sunken vessel of my labor and dreams.

I rode my bike to the boatyard the next day and stood on the shore staring at the half sunken *Yellow Mist*.

"She's a fine boat; you're going to have a lot of fun with her…" I had not noticed the Colonel come up behind me. "… Won't be long before you can start bailing."

Two days later my father, my brothers, and I rowed out to the *Mist* with buckets and started bailing the flooded cabin. It seemed futile at first, but after a half hour, I noticed we were floating a little higher. Excitedly, we bailed faster and faster. Ninety minutes later the bilge was dry and we were floating high and proud. The wooden planks had now swollen and the seams between them had closed and would remain water tight until she was hauled ashore in the fall and dried out while sitting on the cradle all winter.

We put the outboard, gas can, sails, cushions, and various lines aboard and eagerly anticipated Wednesday night when Ed Matthews would give us our first sailing lesson. For three hours we waited excitedly beside the dingy but Ed never showed. My dad went up to the Colonel's house twice and phoned but still no Ed. We were bitterly disappointed. The next day he called and apologized, and we made plans to meet the following Saturday.

The following weekend, Ed was again a no show. He said he was called into work at the last minute. I cannot remember a time in my life when I was more disheartened. My father called Bill Greer, another friend who had sailed years ago but no longer had a boat, and he agreed to teach us the following weekend. I went to the library and found a book on sailing and read it three times. The explanations were not too complicated, even for a twelve-year-old, and it had lots of pictures. I couldn't wait until the following weekend.

"Mike, let's take the *Yellow Mist* for a sail." I said.

"What are you talking about? We don't know how to sail yet."

"I do. I learned from this book I found at the library."

"Dad will kill us if he finds out."

"Don't worry; he's at work. He'll never know."

Three hours later we were sailing back and forth in front of the boatyard screaming with excitement and waving frantically to the Colonel on shore. He wildly waved his arms in encouragement; I think he was more excited than we were. This was better than flying; I was not a passenger in the back seat anymore. I will never know if it was the excitement or the brisk wind stimulating the skin on my face that made my tics worse than ever, but I didn't care. No one except Mike could see me. I had the tiller in my hand, and I was in control; master of the ship. We completely lost track of time.

"Oh, my God, David!"

"What?"

"There is a black car on the end of the dock flashing its lights. I think its dad!"

"It can't be; he's still at work."

"I'm sure it's him. Keep sailing out farther."

The car with the flashing lights did not go away.

"Mike we can't stay out here forever."

As we approached the dock our father, now standing beside the car waving his arms frantically and yelling, was beyond furious.

"What the hell do you think you're doing? Get that boat into the dock right NOW!"

We dropped the sails and glided into the dock. I threw him the line, and then we sat silently in the cockpit staring down and endured his scathing rebuke. He finally calmed down and said, "You have no idea what you are doing. You could have capsized out there."

"No, Dad, it's easy, I learned from a book I got at the library. Get on, I'll show you."

He stepped aboard with some trepidation but fifteen minutes later we were tacking across the bay with the sails billowing, rail down, and my dad with the tiller in his hand, screaming with delight.

Over the next 15 years we would enjoy three successively larger sailboats. They were a major focal point for our family. Later, I would own a series of sailboats, as would my two brothers. Boating remains a major part of our lives to this day. I eventually spent nine years living on the ocean. It was my place of ultimate peace. The sea is nonjudgmental; it does not care if you blink, twitch, jerk, spin, or make n-n-n-noises. It accepts and challenges everyone equally. In the meantime, my dad's words came true: it *kept his boys together a little longer.*

Life ashore was not as kind. In junior high school there were parties and dances to attend but most of the time it was just a bunch of kids hanging out together. The place was not really important. We would go to Annie's Restaurant on Main Street. There were no tables or chairs, just twelve booths arranged in two rows. Although each was meant to seat four, we usually crammed in six to eight. Tony, the overweight owner with a perpetually gravy stained apron, never complained; I guess he was just thankful for the business. In the three years I spent hanging out at Annie's, I don't think I ever heard anyone order anything except "*chips and gravy.*"

The girls would crowd into one booth and the boys into an adjacent one. I was able to blend into the crowd somewhat, so my bizarre facial contractions were less obvious—safety in numbers. I could, for a time, forget my strangeness until someone new joined the group. Then it was just a matter of time before I heard the inevitable whisper, *"What's wrong with him?"* that made me feel alienated and ashamed.

All anyone wants at that age is to fit into a peer group, any group. I yearned to belong somewhere but my strange behavior made it all but impossible. I spent a great deal of time alone, and for most of my young life my only true friends were my family.

CHAPTER FOUR
"THE BITTERSWEET YEARS"

"Next. What's your name?"

"David Bardsley."

"Did Mr. Brown send you here?"

"Yes, ma'am."

"Ok, Mr. Bardsley, start singing from the second verse. Ready? One…two…and three."

I was acutely aware of the forty sets of eyes staring at me. I knew they could feel my terror; they didn't have to look at my sweat-stained shirt for confirmation. The stifled laughter magnified my humiliation tenfold. My twitching and head jerking intensified as they always did during stressful situations. Mrs. Kingston mercifully stopped me half-way through the song.

"Thank you, David. Mr. Alexander told me this morning he still needed help on the stage crew. I'm sure you would be a great asset behind the scenes." She didn't need to add, "Where no one can see you, weirdo;" it was obvious to all.

I attended Saint Francis, an all-boys Catholic high school. The corresponding Catholic girls' school, Saint Jude, was four blocks away. Each year the girls' school asked the boys' school for volunteers to fill the male roles in their annual musical. The turnout that year had been especially dismal so the principal of the girls' school, called Mr. Brown, the principal of the boys' school, and asked if he could somehow encourage more male volunteers. Mr. Brown assembled the entire football team in the gym and then told us in no uncertain terms that each one of us was going to "*volunteer*" for the school musical.

"Mr. Bardsley."

"Yes, sir!" I bellowed out in military fashion, as my teammates snickered.

"The next auditions for the Saint Jude musical are tomorrow at four o'clock. Take this players list when you go to the audition tomorrow and give it to Mrs. Kingston. I want every one of you there, is that understood?"

We nodded in unison.

"Dismissed."

I am sure he would have granted me an exemption had he known the extent of the pain and humiliation I was to suffer.

I reported to Mr. Alexander, as directed, and was most pleased to discover that indeed he was in need of stage hands to move the furniture and sets between scenes. Back in school the next day, I was stopped in the hall by Mr. Brown and he seemed most satisfied when I told him I was taking part in the school musical.

The play ran for two consecutive weekends, and almost everyone agreed that it was the best musical the school had ever presented. A large cast party was planned following the final Saturday night performance; even the stage hands were invited. Somehow, I had mustered the courage to ask the enchanting Melanie Whittaker to go with me. She had done a spectacular job in the supporting lead role and I was shocked when she said, "Yes."

As I drove into the Whittaker's long U-shaped driveway and stopped in front of the palatial house, I felt totally out of place. I was definitely intimidated as I ascended the steps and reached for the ornate door bell. A large robust woman, devoid of any waist and wearing an ankle length floral dress, opened the door.

"Hi, I'm David Bardsley, and I'm here to pick up Melanie."

There was a long, uneasy pause while she inspected me from head to toe.

"Yes, come in," she finally said, breaking the silence. I'm Melanie's mother. She should be down in a moment." Another long pause. "Are you all right?"

I was nervous and this exacerbated my twitching. Most of the time I was unaware of my quirks until someone mentioned them.

"Have a seat. I'll tell her you're here."

I quickly surveyed the room and the large, pillow-filled green velvet sofa looked most inviting. I moved to the far end and sat down.

"*YIPPPP!*"

A screeching, high-pitched yelp filled the air. I immediately leapt to my feet in startled panic. Mrs. Whittaker pivoted in the doorway and streaked back to the sofa. She frantically grabbed the fluffy sofa pillows and threw them to the floor, exposing the tiny Chihuahua, still yelping.

"His leg…my God, you've broken his leg."

She picked up the dog, laid it on one of the pillows, and I could clearly see the left front leg was bent at a very precarious angle; not unlike my arm after the fall from the tree.

"Melanie, get down here *right now*," she screamed.

A few seconds later a startled Melanie appeared in the doorway. She looked adorable. Our eyes met but we did not speak.

"Bring the car to the front door, quickly. We've got to get Tiny to the vet."

Melanie instantly vanished. My copious apologies were falling on deaf ears. I rushed to open the front door for Mrs.

Whittaker as she carried the pillow containing Tiny to the car. As she loaded the dog into the back seat, I heard her ask Melanie and not in a whisper, "What's *wrong* with him?"

I pretended not to hear and asked if I should follow them in my car.

"Definitely *not*," Mrs. Whittaker barked. The car sped out of sight.

Not wanting to go alone, I decided to skip the cast party and just drove around for a very long time. Before heading home, I went down to the football field and ran wind sprints in the dark until I was exhausted. No drug ever made me feel better than vigorous physical exercise. After all, "*The only good boy is a tired boy.*"

I saw Melanie at various functions over the next year or so, but we never had the chance to become more than casual friends. Two years later she died when an enormous log rolled off the truck her car was passing and killed her instantly.

Einstein

Ok, so I was no Einstein, but my grades were better than average; I was a solid B student. On the football field, the track, or the hockey rink, no one cared how much I blinked, twitched, or jerked my head as long as I kept scoring. And score I did. Athletics were my savior, and my joy, and they continue to be to this day. I learned to live with the plethora of broken bones and sports injuries. It was always worth it.

"Sit down, Mr. Bardsley; I have your attendance report for the week here. It seems to be a repetition of the previous weeks. Mr. Hughes, Mr. Long, Mr. Abrams, and Mr. Cole all reported you skipped their classes again. Is this true?"

"Yes, sir."

"Why?"

"I went to gym class, sir."

"Mr. Quinn (the gym teacher) tells me you sometimes attend two or three gym classes a day. Is that true?"

"Yes, sir."

"Why?"

"I can't really explain why. Sometimes I just have to. I feel like I'll explode if I don't."

"Well, if you do it again, *I* am going to explode. You will be suspended; do you understand?"

"Yes, sir."

"Now get back to class."

I did it again and again and was never suspended. I am sure Mr. Quinn was so inwardly delighted that I loved gym so much, he never reported me. Sometimes, after my third gym class of the day he would say, "Ok, Bardsley, that's enough. I know you're supposed to be somewhere else. Now get back to class." Then he would shoot me that quirky little smile and I knew I would not be reported.

If you had a written excuse from your parents stating that you could not attend gym class, for whatever reason, you still had to go to the gymnasium and sit in the bleachers and watch the class for the duration. Most of these kids had nothing wrong with them. I could never understand why they wanted to miss out on all the fun. I thought they were just lazy. Looking back, maybe their lack of athletic ability and "less than perfect" bodies made them feel awkward and embarrassed, just as my tics and twitching did to me.

I was never afraid of Mr. Brown calling my parents. As long as I was attending gym class or some other sports activity they would never be angry with me, especially my father; he understood early on the positive effects vigorous physical activity had on me. Despite this, education was always supremely important in their eyes. I was never pushed into it or lectured about the importance of education. It was much more subtle than that, and deadly effective.

"David, have you given any thought as to which university you would like to attend?"

"University? Dad, I'm only twelve-years old."

"I know son, but it's never too early to start thinking about it."

Not another word on the subject of education would be

mentioned. Then four or five days later, when I least expected it, the same question would be repeated. This continued for three years; then the question abruptly changed.

"David, have you given any thought about which grad school you would like to attend?"

"Grad school? Dad, I'm not even in high school yet."

"I know son, but it's never too early to start thinking about it." Just as suddenly the subject would be dropped, only to be repeated days later.

My all-male high school had three hundred students. Less than twenty percent went on to college. By the time I entered the tenth grade, the thought of not attending university had never occurred to me. My only decision was, *What grad school should I attend?*

As I walked across the brightly lit stage to accept my diploma, I looked out into the darkened crowded auditorium and saw only two faces. They were bursting with pride.

Every school I attended, from primary through high school, had a parents' day. Fewer than half the students had a parent show up and it was always the mother. My father left work and he and my mother spent hours speaking to every teacher. Parents were invited to sit in on classes; none did, except mine.

My classmates would snicker and laugh. "They're Bardsley's parents."

I was so humiliated I would plead with my parents to leave. They never did. It ended with high school…or so I thought.

Following my sophomore year at college I had a summer job in a pathology laboratory and on nice days I would sit outside and enjoy my lunch. I was surprised when my parents' car pulled up. My father rolled down the window and handed me an open envelope, "You did really well. We are so proud of you."

"What? This is addressed to me. It's my transcript. You opened my mail; you can't do that."

"Of course we can; we're your parents; it's our job." As they sped off my father yelled, "There's still room for improvement."

I couldn't stay upset for long. Many of my classmates had no one who cared if they passed of failed. When it came to blinking, twitching, spinning, and blurting God had dealt me a rotten hand; when it came to family, he gave me straight aces.

CHAPTER FIVE
"WHAT IS IT NOW, DAVID?"

"In 1628, the British anatomist William Harvey discovered the circulation of the blood. It starts here in the left side of the heart and goes to the lungs..."

"*Pssssst!*"

"Then the freshly oxygenated blood comes back down here to the right side..."

"*Pssssst!*"

Miss Wilson shot me a riveting glare. "Then through the arterial system..,"

"*Pssssst!*"

She stepped away from the blackboard, walked over to my front row desk, and asked in a muffled, agitated tone, "What is it now, David?"

I whispered as quietly as I could. "It goes the other way; the blood flows the other way. From the right side of the heart to the lungs then back to the left side of the heart."

She spun around and looked at the diagram on the board then went to the lectern and studied her notes for a moment before returning to the board. "Sorry, everyone. What Harvey had discovered was that the blood flows from the right side of the heart, to the lungs, back to the left heart, then to the body."

Miss Wilson was certainly no more than five years older than me; she had long auburn hair pulled back in a tight professional pony tail, a slim body, and beautifully shaped legs. Perhaps that is why I always sat up front. She had finished her master's degree in early European history the previous year and had just secured her first job as assistant professor. We were her first class.

I was in pre-med, a biology and chemistry major, but I needed one history course to obtain my Bachelor of Science degree. I chose History of Science because it was the study of the major scientific discoveries and the geniuses who made them; infinitely more interesting than the Franco Prussian War or early European history. There were forty-one students, eighteen of whom were football players. I learned later they chose this course because new professors are apparently scrutinized very carefully by their department heads and a high failure rate in their first class is not acceptable. They were correct. It was not a challenging course. It was only two weeks later that Miss Wilson committed another faux pas and I quietly corrected her. I knew my physics, biology, and chemistry better than she.

The first day of the second semester started on a tense note. Miss Wilson stormed into the class room carrying a large stack of test papers and slammed them on the table. She stared at the class for a long time without saying a word. It was very uncomfortable.

Finally she spoke. "I want the following people to please stand up."

She read out six names; mine was the last.

"I want to thank you six from the bottom of my heart. Yesterday I went to Dean McLane and handed in my resignation." Tears started to form in her eyes and her voice cracked. "I told him

I'm disillusioned; I'm wasting my time here. You people don't want to learn anything. All you want is a passing grade."

The football players nodded in silent agreement.

"I handed him my resignation, but he convinced me to stick it out until the end of the year and concentrate on the six who passed. Perhaps I can make a difference in their lives. As for the rest of you, you can go to hell!"

Two weeks later I received a note in my box from Miss Wilson asking me to come to her office, which I did the very next day. Sitting there, I felt a little awkward as she thanked me for being one of the six who passed, for caring about her course, and for the help I had given her in class. "Now, there is one other matter I would like to discuss. I know I am not much older than you but I am your professor, I am engaged, and I find your constant winking at me disconcerting and totally inappropriate."

My face exploded with the rush of blood. I was totally mortified. I fumbled with the words, trying to explain I wasn't winking; it was involuntary tics.

What was wrong with me? If I only knew.

I was so embarrassed I never wanted to go back to her class. However, that is not how my parents had taught me to deal with adversity. It took every ounce of courage I could muster to return to class, but from that day on I took my place at the back of the room again, with the dumb football players.

CHAPTER SIX
"ELECTROCUTED"

"I think I would be a great asset, Mr. Black. I have just finished my second year of medical school and I have completed a course in advanced first aid."

I was seated across the desk from George Black, the head of industrial first aid at S.J. Drydock, a large shipyard employing some three thousand men, and I wanted a summer job.

Half of what I said was true. I did have a course in first aid, but I had only completed the second year toward my Bachelor of Science degree. I had been hired two weeks before by the shipyard as a general yard laborer, which meant I toiled eight hours a day at the bottom of a huge dry dock, never seeing the light of day; lugging, toting, pushing, and stacking things while standing knee deep in mud and industrial sludge. It was backbreaking labor, I was constantly filthy, and I wanted something better—much better.

"Well, it looks like you are just the person we need, Doc. I'll call your foreman and have you transferred over here tomorrow."

I loved my new job. I worked the day shift for the first week with two other first aid attendants. Jimmy was a sixty-something Scotsman from Edinburgh, with thin red hair and an accent as thick as his eyebrows. He told a constant stream of stories and jokes that I always laughed at, even if I only understood half the words.

John was a thin, wiry forty-year-old who had little formal education other than industrial first aid. When I met John, he had just returned after being absent for five days. John lived in a small rural town and, like many people in the area, had badly neglected his oral hygiene. Driven by pain, he went to the dentist and was given the grim news about the cost and time required to restore his decaying mouth. He had neither the money nor the desire to proceed. In Canada, medicine is socialized but dentistry is not. John called a country physician, old Doc Turner, the next day and told him the dentist said he needed all his teeth removed.

"Be at my office at six today," was Doc's reply.

Doc Turner's office was on the ground floor of his old rambling farm house and when John arrived Doc was all dressed up in a black tuxedo.

"Sit over in that chair by the lamp," Doc pointed to the corner of the room.

John sat in the old upright kitchen chair as Doc drew some Novocain from a large bottle and proceeded to freeze every inch of John's mouth. Doc disappeared upstairs for fifteen minutes and then returned. He took off his jacket, picked up some forceps, and started pulling. Twenty-five agonizing minutes later he was finished. He put two large pieces of gauze together, folded them in half and stuck them in John's mouth.

"Bite down on this. You feel ok?"

John gave a stunned nod.

"Ok, come on. I'll walk you to your car."

Doc put on his dinner jacket and helped John to his car. No sutures, no pain medication, no antibiotics. One drove home; the other drove to a dinner party. Doc was an MD so this would be covered under the government medical plan; dentists were not covered.

I liked John and Jimmy very much and hated it when they asked me questions about medical school. I had to lie. They always called me Doc. There was a constant stream of patients coming to the clinic with cuts, scrapes, burns, strains, foreign bodies in their eyes, severe hangovers, migraines, and welders flash.

After two weeks I was up to speed, and I took over the graveyard shift, midnight to 8:00am, solo. There was only a skeleton workforce during this shift so I was rarely busy. By 1:30 I would turn the lights out, crawl onto one of the stretchers, and sleep soundly until the day crew woke me. It was a dream job. The workers were always grateful when I treated their wounds, and for one of the first times in my life I felt "important." They never asked about my tics and twitches; they just looked the other way when I caught them staring, like everyone else.

For the last two weeks of the summer, I was switched back to the day shift so Jimmy could go on vacation. A worker John knew by name appeared in the doorway of the clinic with a laceration on his right arm. At first I thought he was drunk. The whole time we were treating his laceration, he was blinking, twitching, and jerking his head back and forth. Then I realized he must be mimicking me and my face turned beet red with embarrassment and shame.

When he left I asked, "Is he always like that?"

"Two years ago he was drilling holes in the bulkhead of a cargo hold," John explained. "He was standing in two inches of water when the electric drill short-circuited, and he was electrocuted. He passed out and fell to the floor unable to let go of the drill. He lay there in the water, convulsing for five minutes before they could shut the electricity off and get to him. A year later he was able to return to work but he was never the same, poor guy."

A week and a half later, on my last day of work, John looked over at me and asked innocently, "Hey Doc, have you ever been electrocuted?"

I was shattered.

CHAPTER SEVEN
"DO YOU HAVE A MATH BRAIN?"

In high school I was a pretty solid student in everything except math. I marveled at how effortless math was for some students, but not for me. Oh, how I struggled. No matter how hard I tried, I just didn't get it. I was not born with a math brain. I was not one of the lucky ones. The funny thing is, no teacher or student ever told me I didn't have a math brain. My parents certainly didn't tell me. I told myself, and I certainly lived up to my expectations. I was appalling at math. I barely squeaked by.

When I enrolled in college the faculty advisor told me that a course in calculus was a requirement for a Bachelor of Science degree. Other students told me how difficult calculus was so, not possessing a math brain, I felt it was in my best interest to put off calculus until my sophomore year.

Twelve months later, as I was registering for my second year, I realized I had not grown a math brain over the summer vacation, so once again I postponed calculus, for the next two years.

When my senior year arrived, my faculty advisor called me into his office and informed me, in no uncertain terms, that without calculus there would be no degree regardless of how many credits I had. One week later I found myself enrolled in Calculus 101, thirty-five freshmen and me.

"Please see, pleeeease see."

Hands shot up everywhere; mine was first. "No, sir, I don't see. Would you please explain how you got from that equation to that solution?"

"Ah, yes. Please see here." He pointed to the equation on the blackboard and then followed the three lines of computations with his index finger, finally pointing at the solution as he repeated, "Please see here." He brushed the chalk from his hands and then stood staring in silence at the thirty-six bewildered, blank-faced students glaring back at him.

His name was Dr. D. P. Chopra. He was from India. We were the first class he had ever taught. The situation was utterly ridiculous. We did not speak Hindi, he did not speak English. After four weeks of this nonsense, the class elected me, the senior, to go to the head of the math department and explain our plight. I called and made an appointment.

The secretary led me to the inner office door and knocked. "Come in," sounded the high pitched male voice from within. She gestured for me to enter.

I pushed the door open and strode in confidently thrusting out my hand. "Good afternoon, sir. My name is David Bard…."

My faced flushed and I instantly had a nauseating feeling in the pit of my stomach. Seated behind a large oak desk, was a very slim, distinguished looking gentleman with a full white beard and atop his aged brown face sat a big white turban. The sign on his desk read: *Dr. Binge Chopra.*

My mind went completely blank as I stared at the sign, but I eventually regained my composure. I explained in great detail our plight. Dr. Chopra listened politely and without interruption until I had finished. Then it was his turn.

"Mr. Bardsley, my youngest son, Dr. D. P. Chopra—your teacher—has just graduated from the most prestigious university in all of India with a degree in advanced theoretical mathematics. I can assure you he is a brilliant mathematician and an excellent teacher. Furthermore, his English is improving rapidly, and you and your classmates should consider yourselves lucky to have him as your teacher. Now if there is nothing else, you may go."

I went back and reported the results of my efforts to my classmates. Things did not improve. They grew worse. At Christmas twenty-nine of the thirty five students failed, including me, and I failed miserably. The six who passed were the lucky ones; apparently they had math brains.

Second term was no better. We banded together into small groups and tried to help one another, but it was no use. I stopped going to class altogether and tried to teach myself from a different textbook, but that also proved hopeless. Seven weeks before the final exam I realized, for the first time, that I was definitely going to fail. A failure in calculus meant no Bachelor of Science degree, no grad school, and no life as I had dreamed it. I became despondent. I woke up two or three times every night thinking about the impending failure and how it would impact my life. I tried to think of what kind of job I could get that would make me happy. Something in the science field, perhaps a lab assistant or a drug salesman. I was truly miserable.

Sitting in the library one night feeling alone and discouraged, I had a revelation. I cannot explain why or how, but I made a decision there and then that I was going to pass calculus. I would make it happen, whatever it took. All of a sudden I had a tremendous feeling of certainty, not hope. I did not know how I was going to accomplish this feat, but I was definitely going to succeed.

We were having a snack in the student union building when my friend Peter pointed out his former classmate. "See that fat guy over there? He was in my math class two years ago and he is brilliant. I swear he knew more than the professor."

A solution hit me. I would find someone really good at math, give them my identification, and pay them to write the final exam for me. I was desperate. I would try anything; even cheat if that was what it was going to take.

Peter agreed to help me. We asked around campus and I was surprised by the difficulty I was having finding someone, regardless of how much money I offered.

Three days later the phone rang and it was Peter. "I've got your boy. He graduated two years ago as a math major and he's going to meet us at the student union building today at four. Don't be late."

I hung up the phone ecstatic. I certainly felt guilty and it went against everything I had been taught but, damn it, the university had to take some responsibility for subjecting us to a teacher who could not communicate in our language. I was justified, or so I tried to convince myself.

Peter and Rob were seated by the vending machines in the student lounge and as I approached Rob looked up. Both of us knew immediately that the plan was not going to work. Despite our weight and frames being similar, Rob had red hair and green eyes. My hair and eyes are brown. We would be caught for sure. We discussed the possibility of him wearing glasses and some kind of hat but since the exam was to be written in early June, wearing a hat inside would probably draw even more attention. I thanked him for his offer and he left.

"Jesus, Pete, what am I going to do? I just can't fail this class."

"Why don't you try getting a tutor?"

"I tried getting help before but it didn't work out."

" No, I mean a real tutor, like a professor or something."

"No one in Dr. Chopra's department is going to go against the old man or his son."

"What about Dalhousie? That school is four times bigger than we are so they must have a huge math department."

Dalhousie was another university on the other side of the city. We were athletic rivals, but otherwise there was not much interaction between the two schools. I had nothing to lose. I called and to my surprise was given an appointment to see Dr. Slone, head of the math department.

He chuckled as I related my story of woe. "Sir, is there any way you or any of your professors could help me? I am desperate."

"David, you don't need the head of the math department or even a professor to tutor you. This is elementary calculus. Any graduate student would be more than qualified. On the way out speak to Sheila, my secretary. She has a list of grad students who do tutoring. Good luck."

I received a list with thirteen names. I rushed home and immediately called the first name on the list, Brad. I was surprised to find him home in the middle of the afternoon.

"How much time do we have until the exam?" he inquired.

"Six weeks."

"What text book are you using?"

"Plank's Calculus."

"I know it well. It has twelve chapters. We can do two chapters a session for the next six weeks and you will be ready."

We agreed on a time, place, and price. I started our first session by explaining to Brad the real problem: I just didn't have a math brain.

"That is the stupidest thing I've ever heard anyone say! If you have a brain, then you have a math brain. Everyone does."

I wanted to respond, "Easy for you to say, nerd." but I held my tongue.

Brad asked me a few questions and he quickly realized I knew almost nothing about calculus. "No problem. We'll start here; chapter one, page one."

We started slowly and he made sure I understood thoroughly before moving on to the next section. Ninety minutes later we were finished and I was assigned eight problems as homework before the next session.

The following day I opened the text and started in on the first problem. When I had finished, I rushed to the back of the book, where the solutions were listed, to see if my answer was correct. To my great surprise and joy, it was.

Bolstered by my newfound confidence I tackled the second problem. Same result. Forty minutes later I had completed the assignment and got six of the eight answers correct. I was hopeful.

The following session with Brad went smoothly. Looking back, he was certainly the best teacher I ever had. Step by methodical step he built a solid calculus foundation for me. Again he assigned eight problems as homework. This time I just knew by the process that the solutions had to be right. Unlike before, I did not have to rush to the back of the textbook to check if the answers were correct. My confidence soared.

By the end of the fifth session we had completed the entire text, one week ahead of schedule.

"You don't need me anymore," Brad said. "You have a very good understanding of the basics of calculus. You will do just fine on the exam. Call me if you get stuck."

During that final week I was preparing for five different exams. Normally, I would take a break every two hours and have something to drink or take a short walk, but now I found myself reaching for the calculus book. I would flip it open and solve a problem or two. They became like crossword puzzles or games; they were fun and completely took my mind off whatever subject I was studying.

I don't know what possessed me, but I would look around in study hall and if no one was close by, I would put my finger against one nostril to distort my voice and say, "*Dr. Bardsley, Dr. Bardsley, paging Dr. Bardsley.*" That fantasy made me feel fantastic, and the better I felt, the more diligently I applied myself to my studies.

The mark on that final calculus exam was the highest I scored in twelve years of university. The overall mark was diluted when the Christmas exam was factored in, but it was easily good enough for me to graduate with a Bachelor of Science degree and be accepted into graduate school. The dream was still alive.

I have often thought how different my life might have been had I cheated, and am so thankful I did not. I would have robbed myself of the opportunity to believe in my abilities. It was an enormous breakthrough for me. My parents had told me a thousand times throughout my childhood, "You are David Bardsley, and you can do or be anything you want."

Until then, they were words I wanted to believe, but now I did believe them. I realized, for the first time, that with ordinary talents and extraordinary persistence you can accomplish anything. Learn the basics well and then build from there. Ordinary is all you need to succeed.

I consider myself blessed because throughout those oh so difficult early years, my parents constantly gave me the gift of these four magic words, *"We believe in you."* After years and decades of hearing this, the magic started to work and the words became, *"I believe in me."*

CHAPTER EIGHT
"AWAKENING THE FIRE WITHIN"

Whap!

I felt the sting on my face. My head jolted to the side, and I was stunned for a moment. I did not see his hands move; then I realized it must have been his foot. Enraged, I charged towards his diminutive frame.

Whap! Whap!

This time I saw his hands coming, but by the time the thought registered in my now rattled brain, it was too late to do anything. His fists bounced off my chest in rapid succession.

"Hia!" He bowed and stepped back.

This was my first meeting with Eric Lim. I had come to the karate demonstration at the urging of my friend Darren. I had no idea I was going to end up being part of it. Eric and I were both juniors at the same university and that is where the similarity ended.

He was an Asian from Hong Kong, had a black belt in karate, and weighed a sleek one hundred and thirty pounds.

I was a thick white guy from Canada and tipped the scales at one hundred ninety. My lifelong hyperactivity and obsession with vigorous physical activity assured none of it was fat.

I was shocked at the speed and power of his blows. I immediately became a disciple. For the next year I trained with Eric three times a week and still kept up with my full complement of other sports, but this quickly became my favorite. My facial twitches and head jerks only served to confuse my opponents and for the first time in my life my "weirdness" was an advantage. An advantage I would have gladly relinquished; if only I could.

Eric returned to Hong Kong after he graduated. I moved on to graduate school and joined a new karate club in town where Jim Marks, the sensei, would become my new mentor. Under his guidance I would eventually achieve my highest level in any sport.

***

I had always enjoyed science and thought medicine would be perfect for me. Our family physician, Dr Donner, had six children. His son Bruce had been one of my best friends when we were children. I often played at their house but Dr. Donner was seldom around. He was always working.

In junior high I played on the same soccer team as Bill Gibson whose father was a dentist. Dr. Gibson attended every practice, every game, and every school function. He seemed to have lots of free time. Their home was every bit as nice as Dr. Donner's, and Dr. Gibson drove a BMW. From a pure science point of view, I naively thought the two professions were very similar and the advantages of dentistry seemed obvious.

"Well, Mr. Bardsley, I have been looking over your file and you seem to have done very well for yourself. The next four years will not be easy but if you apply yourself diligently and stay out of trouble, I am sure you will become an excellent dentist. If you run into problems don't hesitate to come and see me. Welcome to Dalhousie University. Do you have any questions?"

"No, sir. Thank you, Dean Robertson."

I was euphoric. My goal of becoming a dentist was about to begin. Fortunately for me, the application process to dental school did not involve a pre-admission interview. Only transcripts of previous grades and personal letters of recommendation were required. I have little doubt I would have been rejected had it been necessary to sit in front of a selection committee and allow them to observe my strange facial tics, head jerks, and contortions. It did not matter now; I was in.

The class was small, only twenty-five students, so they combined us with the one hundred medical students for the first two years. It was a gratifying time in my life. My strangeness was somewhat accepted by my fellow students, and although the work load was heavy, I loved it. During those first two years we studied all the basic medical sciences: pharmacology, microbiology, pathology, anatomy, physiology, etc. No more dissecting frogs and fish; we had cadavers. This was the real thing.

Academically, I was always in the top third of my class, but still I enjoyed a great social life. My status as a dental student served me well in the social hierarchy of the university, especially with the undergraduate females.

The bottom fell out in year three. We were split off from the medical students and our education as dentists began. I hated it. I found nothing interesting about teeth. When would I get to use all that medical science I just spent years learning? Never! It was a rude awakening.

I struggled through that first semester. We had a twelve-day Christmas break and my ski buddy Pat and I packed all our gear into my yellow Volkswagen beetle and headed to Montreal, a fifteen-hour drive. Our destination was Mount Tremblant, a ski area about an hour north of the city. Pat knew the assistant ski school director from his boyhood days in Montreal. We had made arrangements to work as ski instructors over the busy holiday break. I spoke no French.

The next morning we went to pick up our passes and identification. Our pictures were taken with a Polaroid camera, and after asking me to spell my name three times, the ski company secretary disappeared into the back office and emerged twenty minutes later with our passes.

"Here you go, *Monsieur Barnsloui.*"

I inspected the pass and sure enough under my picture was the name, *David Barnsloui.*" I explained the error to her and repeated my name several more times. She took a new picture and disappeared into the inner office. After twenty minutes she emerged with a huge, satisfied smile and handed me the new pass which read, *David Barnsloui.*

I thanked her in French, and we left. The name stuck; it was probably five years before my friends stopped calling me Barnsloui. What followed were ten of the happiest days of my life. I skied every day and was paid for it. Room and board were included and most of the students in my class were young American girls from New York there on vacation and more intent on enjoying the night life than learning how to ski.

I quickly learned that a ski instructor's responsibility does not end when the lifts close. I was in heaven. Two days before the job was to end, the ski school director offered Pat and me full-time positions for the season. After lengthy discussions, Pat decided to return to school, but I decided to stay. I hated dentistry, so the decision was easy. I would enjoy my new found status as a ski instructor and then see about applying to medical school for the following year.

I was seated in the dining room of the ski lodge enjoying dinner and the camaraderie of my fellow instructors when I was told there was a phone call for me in the office. *Who could it be? It must be Pat;* he had returned to school and he was the only one who knew I was still there.

"David, this is Dean Robertson. I just called your parents and they gave me this number. They were as surprised as I am that you are not back in class. Are you ill?"

A long conversation ensued while I explained my joy during the first two years with the medical students but my disappointment and disillusionment about dentistry.

"I thought I would teach skiing for the rest of the year and then apply to medical school in the fall."

"I understand completely" said the dean. "If you come back and start the second term, I will speak to the dean of medicine and we will see what kind of advanced placement can be arranged so you don't have to start all over again. Does that seem fair?"

"I will be there by Monday, Dean."

I returned as promised and endured the first month; then something happened that would change my life forever. During the second half of the third year, every dental student had to go to the hospital for two weeks and rotate through the oral and maxillofacial surgery department. We did not get to do much, just observe and assist. We did, however, get to go to the operating room and scrub in on all the major cases.

This was definitely not dentistry. Cutting and suturing, sawing bones, manipulating entire jaws, wiring and pinning fractures—I had hit the jackpot. By the third day I knew exactly what I wanted to do for my life's work. I made my intentions known to the head of the surgery department and he advised me that the fastest way to be accepted into the surgery program would be to finish dentistry and do a one-year hospital internship and then apply.

I returned to dental school two weeks later with a completely different attitude. I told everyone, including the professors, of my new plans. Minor oral surgery is taught in dental school but this consists of extracting a few teeth and doing the occasional biopsy. The nurse, Mrs. Holly, would screen the prospective surgery patients for the dental students and anything that was remotely difficult was referred out.

I lived for surgery days. I would take on the most challenging cases they would allow me. I quickly became proficient and soon earned a reputation. It was not long before Mrs. Holly was screening difficult cases specifically for me. Most of the students were quite squeamish about surgery. The instructors, all oral and maxillofacial surgeons, would frequently have to coax a frightened dental student into picking up a scalpel and cutting living tissue.

Not me; I believed I could do anything. (*Heart transplant? Sure, I can do a heart transplant.*)

The normal procedure was for the student to examine the patient, decide what was to be done, and then present the case to the surgeon. The surgical instructor would then come to the cubicle and examine the patient to decide whether the student should proceed or not. The surgical instructors were delighted by my enthusiasm and desire to be one of them. Most of the time I would present my case, and they would say, "Go ahead, Mr. Bardsley. Call me when you are finished."

At the beginning of the second term of my final year, I wrote to all the oral and maxillofacial training programs in North America. Many would not even send me the application as I was still a dental student. Every program had an admission requirement of a one-year hospital internship or two years in private general practice.

The head of the surgery department at the Dalhousie Faculty of Dentistry, where I was a student, and the head of the maxillofacial surgery program at Victoria General Hospital, were one and the same: Dr. Frank Covey. He liked me. A letter of recommendation from Dr. Robertson, the dean of dentistry, and Dr. Covey, the head of the surgery department at the dental school, were required for all the maxillofacial programs I was applying to. I applied to nineteen programs even though most told me not to bother, as I was not yet qualified. The Dean and Dr. Covey were extremely annoyed at all the letters of recommendation they had to write on my behalf but I persisted.

Dr. Covey summoned me to his office. "What is wrong with you? Why don't you just follow the rules and do a one-year internship or go into private practice for two years and then apply?"

"Sir, I hate dentistry; it would just be a waste of my time. I would rather go and sell life insurance or something for two years and then say I was in private practice and apply."

"Well, you are wasting everyone's time applying to my program."

"Well, I'm going to apply anyway, sir."

He was becoming visibly annoyed. "What don't you understand? I am chief of the department at Victoria General Hospital and head of the selection committee, and I'm telling you that you will not be accepted until you are fully qualified. Besides, even if you were qualified, there is only one position per year open in our program and we have already accepted the candidate for the upcoming year."

I was greatly disappointed by this news and by the series of rejection letters I received from the other programs during the following weeks. Still, undeterred, once a week I would drop in and see Dr. Covey and discuss my intentions of becoming an oral and maxillofacial surgeon. I later learned that everyone in this profession felt a great dissatisfaction with dentistry and gravitated toward surgery. On one visit, I jokingly told him my father would have a swimming pool built in his backyard if he would let me into the program.

"I already have one," was his humorless reply.

Six weeks before final exams I received a notice to attend a meeting of the surgery department at Victoria General Hospital. All five staff members were there.

"Take a seat, David. We have been discussing your case at great length. We all agree you are a royal pain in the ass, but we have never seen anyone with your burning desire to become an oral and maxillofacial surgeon. We have decided to drop the one year internship or two year private practice requirement and admit you directly to the program.

"As you know we have already accepted a candidate, so for the first time ever, there will be two of you starting at the same time. We are not sure how this will work out; we will have to see as things go along. All of this, of course, is dependent on you maintaining your grades and graduating next month."

I raced from the meeting to the nearest phone and called my parents; for once I knew before they did. I expected them to be ecstatic.

"We expected it would happen. We believe in you," was their calm reply to my fantastic news.

Three days later I boarded a plane and flew to Boston with the rest of the team to participate in the New England kickboxing championships. I had won several local championships and the other dental students and staff knew of my success in this sport, which had become my full-blown passion.

I had been told by Dean Robertson himself to give up the sport. "David, don't be stupid. Boxing and dentistry don't mix; your hands are your livelihood."

I had no idea what was causing my tics, twitches, and head jerks but I did know one thing: physical exercise made the whole thing so much better. Of course, I ignored his advice.

Half my life would pass before I learned that vigorous physical activity is the only known modality that not only increases, but more importantly balances, not one, not two, not three, but all sixty of the known neurotransmitters and it releases a cascade of neuronal growth factors that change the very infrastructure of the brain. Whatever my brain was lacking exercise seemed to provide. It was my mental health steroid.

When Winning Is Losing

"Throw *the bomb*, throw *the bomb*, damn it! You're losing. Throw *the fucking bomb*."

I was slumped on my stool in the corner of the ring, my chest heaving and the searing pain of exhaustion in my lungs. I was dazed and barely aware of my trainer Jimmy screaming in my face.

"Seconds out," yelled the referee.

Jimmy pushed me upwards as he snatched the stool from underneath. I stumbled to the center of the ring to meet my old nemesis, Darren Yee. I had lost to Darren twice before in the quarter finals of the New England middleweight kickboxing championship and now, with one round to go in the championship fight, I was losing again. Darren's kicks were much quicker and more accurate than mine, but our hand speed was about the same. My only advantage was my superior punching power and I had one weapon, my overhand right, The Bomb."

If I landed it, you were going down no matter what. Problem was, I didn't land it often enough. We pummeled away on one another for the next few minutes and then I heard both our corners yell, "30 seconds."

Every fighter has his signature move or favorite weapon and most fighters telegraph it; Darren was no exception. My facial twitches, contortions and head jerks, on the other hand, were completely erratic; even I didn't know when or where they would occur and this served me well in the ring. My opponents never knew when the overhand right was coming. I saw Darren gather himself to throw his signature spinning back kick, and as always he telegraphed it.

I had seen him land it many times before. If it connected, my head would probably come off. But I knew all I had to do was time it perfectly, take a half-step back, and it would wiz by inches from my face. In doing so, however, I would put myself out of reach to launch any counter-attack. Time would run out, and I would lose the championship for the third time. My only hope was to lunge forward, throw *the bomb*, and hope it landed milliseconds before Darren's kick did.

My next recollection was standing in the middle of the ring, shaking my aching right hand, trying to make the pain go away.

"…7, 8, 9, 10."

I did not realize what had happened until the referee grabbed my arm and raised it in victory. From the corner of my eye, I saw Darren struggling to lift himself off the canvas. Jimmy jumped into the ring and lifted me up. My teammates swarmed the ring as I pumped my fists into the air. In all of the sports in which I have participated, this was my finest moment. I was the New England middleweight kickboxing champion. I would never rise to that level in any sport again.

We celebrated long and hard that night despite my throbbing hand. Early the next morning the whole team stumbled onto the plane for our flight back to Canada.

As I sat on the plane, my now grossly swollen right hand throbbed and turned darker and darker as I watched. I could barely move my fingers. Something was wrong. When we landed I went straight to emergency. It was late Sunday evening and after what seemed like an endless wait, the doctor pulled back the curtain, stepped into the cubicle, and placed the x-ray film on the view box.

"The fingers are fine, but you can see clearly the fracture through these two metacarpals."

"Does it need pinning?"

"No, they are pretty well aligned so I think six weeks in a cast should suffice, I'll have the nurse take you down to the casting room."

There was little sleep that night, and it wasn't due to the pain. I was unable to quiet the self talk racing in my wind-milling brain. How was I going to fulfill my clinical requirements and graduate from dentistry on time? My right hand was broken. While the first two years of dental school are virtually all academic, the last two years are heavily weighted toward clinical practice. Every student had to demonstrate a *clinical proficiency* in each of these areas and this had to be verified by the chief instructor in each of the disciplines.

I arrived early at the clinic Monday morning. I had another student help me stretch a rubber glove over the bulbous cast on my right hand. Mrs. Higgins, the nurse, seated the first patient in my cubicle. I had just begun an oral examination when Nurse Higgins reappeared.

"Mr. Bardsley, Dean Robertson wants to see you in his office, immediately."

"Is it broken?" queried the Dean.

"Just a little bit; a tiny fracture really."

"I see. Well, that is most unfortunate because I don't want you anywhere near the clinic floor until your hand is completely healed. Is that understood?"

"Yes, sir."

"You obviously will not be able to fulfill your clinical requirements in time for graduation next month, so you will have to return for the summer and hopefully you can graduate in the fall."

I could not believe the terrible turn of events. One week before, my dream had come true; against all odds I was accepted into an oral and maxillofacial surgery program. They had even changed the rules for me! Now everything was ruined. My roommate, Wayne, and I went out that night and got drunk—very drunk.

On Saturday, one week after the cast had been put on; I went to the hardware store and purchased a hack saw blade. I went home and started sawing. It took nearly two hours of meticulous cutting to slice the cast from one end to the other with only minimal damage to my skin underneath. I tried to pry it open and remove my hand but it was impossible so I started making a second cut on the opposite side. Two more hours passed before the cast finally came off in two perfect halves.

The swelling and most of the discoloration were gone. I filled the sink with warm water and immersed my hand, then started opening and closing my fist. Although initially painful, after ten or fifteen minutes it felt remarkably better. I repeated this procedure every two hours all day Saturday and Sunday. At night I would put the two halves of the cast back on my hand and tape them together.

I stayed home Monday and continued the procedure. The next day I went to the dental school and straight up the stairs to Dean Robertson's office.

"Sir, I have just come from the doctor. He took another x-ray and said my hand looks fine."

I held up my castless arm and showed him how well I could move my fingers. "He re-examined the original x-ray and feels it was more of a sprain than a fracture; he said I am good to go."

"That is great news Mr. Bardsley, but I will need a letter from him stating you are completely healed."

"Certainly, I will go back to his office tomorrow and get it."

My dexterity was not anywhere close to what it should have been, so for the next week I filled my clinical time with the most minor procedures I could. As soon as I left the school I would tape the cast back in place. The letter from the fictitious doctor was never mentioned again. I was back in the game. The dream was still alive.

I will always be grateful to my professors in dental school for the compassion and fairness they showed me. They understood what a wonderful opportunity I had been given and my entire surgical future hinged on me graduating on time. My academic grades were good, but my clinical proficiency in dentistry was definitely subpar. They realized that as an oral and maxillofacial surgeon I would never place a filling, make a crown, or perform a root canal. Each one signed me off as clinically proficient. I graduated with the rest of my class and had a two-week vacation before my surgery training began.

Whenever difficulty and discouragement entered my life I would always turn to my parents for support and encouragement. They never once failed to provide it.

I believe it was Viktor Frankl who once said, "You can change the course of a person's life simply by believing in them, even if they are unaware of your belief." I was always aware of my parent's belief in me.

Colliding Worlds

I entered a program that combined a residency in oral and maxillofacial surgery with a simultaneous Master of Science degree. The master's degree is another feather in your cap if you want to teach or do research, which I thought I would like to do. The work load was enormous but I loved it. When you begin university in Canada at the bachelor level, you are required to take courses in which you may have no interest (like calculus) but they are requirements. The further along the academic road you progress, the more freedom you have to choose the course of study you are interested in. At this stage, learning becomes a pleasure.

The incredible demand on my time necessitated giving up most of my sports activities. Only kickboxing remained. It provided an intense physical workout demanding strength, cardiovascular fitness, flexibility, balance, and coordination, but most of all it was a marvelous vent for my hyperactivity. It required little equipment, was a year-round sport, could be done anywhere, and was an amazing confidence builder.

I will never know whether I was good at it because I loved it so much, or if I loved it because I was naturally good at it. It didn't matter. It was exactly what I needed: an extremely efficient method of tiring myself out. And when I did, my strange symptoms subsided and life was better. My father was right again, *"The only good boy is a tired boy."*

Thirteen months after the hand episode, I found myself once again on a plane to Boston to participate in a large east coast tournament. Each fight only lasted three rounds but in large tournaments it was often necessary to fight five or six times over a two-day period to win your weight division. The finals were usually held on Saturday night.

I barely heard the buzzer signaling the last thirty seconds of the fight. I didn't have to. I knew instantly by the look of desperation and panic on my opponent's face. I was ahead on points and we both knew it. His eyes were all whites and he snorted loudly before he charged like a bull across the ring, bent on rendering me unconsciousness. Blows to the groin were not allowed in competition but in the ring, reflexes rule. I had practiced my favorite self-defense move a thousand times: a short, powerful kick to the attacker's groin followed by a thunderous right hand (the bomb) to the side of the head. My signature move.

This combination had no place in the ring but my opponent's frightening charge initiated a reflex I was powerless to stop. I kicked his groin harder than I had ever kicked any human being or training dummy. A loud abrupt groan was released from his barrel chest as he doubled at the waist. His momentum propelled him as he stumbled toward me. He was half way to the canvas when my overhand right (the bomb) lashed out and caught him squarely on the left temple. Now unconscious, he continued falling toward me, much as I would imagine the Leaning Tower of Pisa might fall.

I stepped backwards to clear a path for his descent to the canvas. But I was not quick enough. His huge torso landed on my lead left leg, which was still extended in front of me. I went to the canvass with him. For a moment, the two of us lay motionless. My hands and arms were free so I reached down, grabbed him by the shoulders and rolled him off my legs. Despite knowing I would probably be disqualified by the groin kick, I leapt to my feet to pump my fists in the air in victory, but in that instant I crashed back down to the canvas. I quickly tried to get up, only to crash to the canvas again. As I lay there I glanced down at my feet. I was momentarily bewildered; something did not look right. I could clearly see the front of my left shin and below that my heel.

It's backwards, I thought, as the first wave of white hot pain hit.

Forty-five minutes would pass before the ambulance carrying me arrived at the Boston City Hospital Emergency Department. After I gave what seemed like every conceivable detail of my life to the demanding clerk my stretcher was rolled against a corridor wall, and I was promptly forgotten about. It was obviously a very busy emergency department, and I tried my hardest not to be one of those demanding patients I had so learned to despise, but the pain was becoming unbearable.

"Nurse. Nurse. Please, I need some help over here."

"We'll be with you soon. It's Saturday night, and we're swamped."

I dug my fingernails into the palm of my hands and tried to focus on that pain instead of my leg. My next memory is of a tall, thin young doctor exiting from a room fifty feet away. He was dressed in head-to-toe white, obviously a fellow resident.

"Doctor, please, may I speak to you for a moment?"

The gods were smiling on me. His nametag read "*Dr. John Rent, Orthopedic Resident.*"

"Hi, I'm David Bardsley and, like you, I'm a surgery resident. I'm visiting from Canada and I fractured my leg an hour and a half ago in a kickboxing tournament. I'm in agony. I know you are very busy, but could you please order a narcotic while I am waiting here?"

"Has anyone examined you? Have you been to x-ray yet?"

"No, nothing."

"Shit."

Fifteen minutes later I was lying comfortably on the x-ray table. Not only had I been examined but I had one hundred milligrams of Demerol on board. Life was good again. The radiograph confirmed an incomplete fracture of the tibia and complete fracture of the fibula with full dislocation of the foot.

A few minutes later I was wheeled back to a treatment room in the emergency department. A short time later Dr. Rent appeared with an older gentleman who he introduced as Dr. John Chandler, the orthopedic surgeon on call. Dr. Chandler took over.

"David, unfortunately the operating rooms are very busy and all the anesthesiologists are tied up. It will be at least three hours before we can get you up there. Every minute that the dislocation remains unreduced, the greater the likelihood that surgery will be the only option."

"So, what are you suggesting?"

"We can put a tourniquet just above your knee, and then do an intravenous Novocain drip. This will produce some anesthesia so we can reduce the fracture and dislocation right now."

"But the Novocain will only give anesthesia of the soft tissue and not the bone."

"Yes, but it's better than nothing."

The Demerol was in charge of my brain. "I'm not sure. I would like to make a phone call before I make the decision."

My sister-in-law was from Boston and her mother, Mary, had been a head nurse for decades in numerous Boston area hospitals. They brought a phone over to the stretcher. I called Mary and explained what was happening.

"Mary, do you know who is the best orthopedic surgeon working out of this hospital?"

"No, I haven't worked there for years but I can find out and call you right back."

Five minutes later Dr. Chandler reappeared in the doorway "We are running out of time. What do you want to do?"

Surgeons are like any other professionals; there are some very good ones and some very bad ones. Despite my head swimming from the Demerol, I was frightened. Which group did these people belong to?

"Ok, I guess I should go with the IV block and get it done now." I muttered nervously.

The tourniquet was applied to my leg to keep the intravenous Novocain from spreading to the rest of my body. During the ten minutes it took for the Novocain to drip into my leg, I agonized over whether I was doing the right thing. Then the phone rang and the nurse carried it over to me. It was Mary.

"David, the man you want is Dr. J.P. Chandler. Insist on him and wait as long as necessary for him to get there. Don't let anyone else work on you."

I grinned as I handed the phone back to the nurse.

A few minutes later both doctors reappeared. They pricked the skin on my leg to ensure the block was working.

"David, do you mind if Dr. Rent does the reduction?"

I wanted to say, *of course I mind*. He could damn well practice on someone else, but I too, was a resident, and he had been very kind to me. Without him I probably would still be waiting at the side of the corridor.

"Sure, no problem."

Then Dr. Chandler did something strange. He stacked six wooden tongue depressors, one on top of the other and wrapped several pieces of gauze around them. He handed them to me. "Put this in your mouth. Grab hold of the side rails and when we start the reduction, bite down as hard as you can."

"Ha, ha, but excuse me if I don't think that's very funny."

"It is not meant to be, David. Trust me, it will help."

I did as instructed and felt nauseated as I looked down seeing my knee, shin and heel all in perfect alignment.

"Ready?"

As the searing pain shot up my leg, my teeth sunk into the stack of tongue depressors and I squeezed the side rails so hard my arms seemed to be convulsing. In a matter of seconds it was over. The pain immediately began to dissipate and when I looked down I saw my toes pointing proudly forward.

"Looks good. We will move you down to the plaster room, get a cast on this ASAP, and then take a radiograph to check the alignment."

A wave of relief and relaxation flooded over my body. Then it happened. Without any warning the foot spontaneously and abruptly dislocated. The severely spastic muscles had pulled it back out of place. My heel was once again pointing forward. I screamed.

"Hold on." Dr. Chandler yelled.

I did not even have time to put the tongue depressors between my teeth. Dr. Chandler grabbed the foot and with one mighty pull and twist sent it back into position and held it there. They taped it to the stretcher rail and off we went to the casting room.

"I want you to keep this elevated for five days. See an orthopedic surgeon when you get home and have them change this to a walking cast in ten days. Good luck!"

The next morning I boarded the plane for the two-hour flight back to Canada. I was hoping the seat in front of me would be empty so I could push the seatback forward and elevate my leg, but the flight was full. I could feel the pressure building under the cast shortly after we took off.

Over the next two hours I watched in horror as my toes turned black. The pressure continued to build and the pain intensified. I had seen dry gangrene before and I started to panic. I hobbled to the back of the plane and lay on the galley floor with my leg propped up against the bulkhead. The condition worsened. The flight attendant gave me a knife from one of the meal trays and I tried to cut away at the cast to relieve the pressure but it was useless. Finally the plane touched down. The flight crew made an announcement and the others passengers waited as I deplaned first.

My teammates took care of my luggage and I grabbed the first cab in line and sped toward the Victoria General, my hospital. I did not bother to report to reception. The first nurse who saw me recognized the urgency of the situation when I pointed to my black toes. Within minutes I was in the plaster room watching the technician saw the cast from my leg. An orthopedic consult followed and it was decided the cast would be left off and I was to return the next morning. If there was any evidence of tissue death from gangrene, a series of *dives* would be arranged in the decompression chamber, the same apparatus used by divers to treat the bends. This forces more oxygen into the blood and helps minimize tissue death. I wanted to keep my toes, all of them.

I spent that night with my leg in extreme elevation. By the morning some of the swelling had subsided and the tissue looked healthier. Three days later a new cast was applied.

I hobbled on crutches for the next ten days but was able to perform most of my duties. Working inside the operating room was the biggest challenge. After scrubbing and gowning, you are only considered sterile from the waist up. I found a stool with rollers which was the perfect height. I cut away some of the cast around the back of my knee so I could comfortably bend my leg ninety degrees and kneel the leg on top of the stool. I could then propel myself around the O.R. by pushing with my other leg. I looked silly but it was functional.

I received a scathing rebuke from Dr. Covey and the rest of the surgery staff, and I promised to give up kickboxing. Which I did…at least, until the leg was completely healed.

CHAPTER NINE
"EASY MONEY"

Surgery residents received a very small salary. It would not have been enough to live on had we not received free meals at the hospital cafeteria and had our uniforms supplied. The hospital was large, over one thousand beds, so the cafeteria was open twenty-four hours a day. My apartment was close by and many nights I walked to the hospital, even though I was not on duty, just to get something to eat.

I was concurrently enrolled in a Master of Science program, because I thought it would be beneficial if I ever decided to teach or do research. It was a mistake. The thesis is the focus of any graduate program. The regular graduate students dedicated the bulk of their time to it and the faculty advisors expected nothing less. They seemed completely oblivious to the fact that I was spending an additional fifty to sixty hours a week at the hospital in a residency program. I had chosen to do my research and thesis on blood clotting: the factors that caused premature dissolution of the clot and how this affected the normal healing process.

Due to the nature of my research, I was assigned to the graduate department of physiology and a PhD, Dr. Lenard Marks, was my faculty advisor. During our first meeting he gave the green light to proceed with my proposed research project, which was to be carried out over the next eight months. Graduate students were expected to meet monthly with their advisor to discuss the progress of the research.

Dr. Marks and I got off to a very bad start as I constantly needed to cancel meetings due to my surgery commitments. He never understood my surgical duties and was continually irritated with me. The actual writing of the thesis and not the research itself is certainly the most difficult part. My thesis was designed to consist of six chapters and I was expected to have Dr. Marks approve each one before moving on to the next. I dropped off the first eighteen pages of text to his secretary and made an appointment to see him the following week, an appointment I had to cancel at the last minute. Two weeks later I sat at his desk.

He commenced his assault. "This is absolutely terrible. I think I made more than ten pages of corrections and suggestions. Here, take this thesis by one of my other graduate students and read it. You will see how it should be done."

I looked at my work as I walked home. Every page was covered in red ink. I would have to start all over again. Where would I ever find the time? Our next meeting was in three weeks and as usual I procrastinated. I vowed to spend every spare moment of that next week rewriting the thesis. I dragged my exhausted body home from the hospital each day intent on working on the thesis but it was impossible. I thought of calling Dr. Marks and rescheduling but I knew he would be furious. I took the eighteen pages to the typist and asked her to retype it even though I had not made any of the changes Dr. Marks had suggested. A compete duplicate of my original, minus all the red ink. I arrived at the meeting exactly on time.

I was so nervous that my twitching, blinking and head jerks must have looked like a full blown seizure.

"Sir, I took your advice and made all the corrections you suggested. You were right; it presents much better in the new format." I handed him the folder.

"Take a seat while I read this."

My brow was wet with perspiration; my heart was pounding in my chest. *How could I be so stupid and do such a thing? I deserved everything I was about to get.*

He finished reading, slowly put down the papers, and looked me straight in the eye. I wanted to scream and explain what tremendous pressure I was under at the hospital. I was filled with dread and shame.

"Now why didn't you do this in the first place? Just do the same thing for the next five chapters, and you will have a thesis."

I was dumbfounded. I left his office in a daze but I had learned a valuable lesson. After each of our five successive meeting, I would thank Dr. Marks for his valuable suggestions, and then have the original retyped with few, if any, of the changes he had suggested. At the subsequent meeting I would present it as though all the changes he suggested had been made. My thesis was eventually signed off, and I defended it successfully but it gave me little satisfaction. I knew what I had done was wrong.

***

"David, I clipped a piece out of the local paper and mailed it to you. Make sure you read it."

"What is it about?

"Just read it when it arrives."

Three days later I received the article my father had mailed. It was titled, "The Leonard and Catherine O'Brien Scholarship Foundation." They were offering non-repayable fellowships to graduate students pursuing any area of research. What did I have to lose? I sure needed the money, so I wrote for an application. I took great care in explaining my area of research and how it involved placing synthetic biodegradable cotton, soaked with topical thrombin, a protein necessary for the blood clotting process, into surgical wounds and studying the effect on wound healing. Five weeks later I received a reply stating that I was one of the finalists and should appear before the selection committee the following month.

I was a wreck when I arrived in Fredericton for the interview. I had been on call all night and I had just driven three hundred miles, but my nervousness kept me awake and alert. *Why couldn't they do this be telephone? What will they think when they see me twitching and blinking? I am sure the other candidates are a whole lot smarter than me. I don't stand a chance.*

Finally my name was called. We were informed beforehand who was on the committee; nonetheless I was startled to see five such prominent people seated behind a long table ready to interview me. The retired university president, the wealthy industrialist, and the lawyer I recognized from their pictures in the newspaper and TV. The other two I knew by name only. After brief introductions they asked me to explain my research, which I did succinctly and methodically, then waited for questions.

The university president started. "So you are transplanting this tissue into another person and studying how they heal?"

I was momentarily stunned by the question. *Transplant? Did they not listen to a word I just said? I am not transplanting anything.*

"Well sir, the topical thrombin is separated from donated blood and then carried to the surgical site on a synthetic fiber that the body adsorbs over time and…"

The industrialist cut in before I could finish. "So you transplant this thrombin from the blood of one person to another and study the effect of the transplant on healing, is that correct?"

Suddenly it struck me. For the past six months the media was all abuzz with the stories of the latest heart transplants. There were daily news updates on the miraculous new transplant procedures and on the progress of the recipients. Transplants seemed to be the cutting edge of the latest medical technology. I immediately told them what they wanted to hear.

"That is exactly correct, sir. I am *transplanting* the thrombin from the donor to the recipient and studying the effects of the *transplant* on healing."

That was all they needed. There were no more questions. I got into my Volkswagen and drove the three hundred miles home, arriving at four thirty a.m. Just enough time to eat, shower, and make it to the hospital on time for my six a.m. shift. A congratulatory letter from the selection committee and the first of two large checks arrived one month later.

Thirty years would pass before I was once again honored, as the first recipient of the "Leonard and Catherine O'Brien Scholarship."As I stood in the banquet hall and looked out over the gathering of accomplished past and present scholarship recipients, I could not help but think, *"Where is the award for those who loved us and sacrificed to get us here—our parents."*

"Cocaine"

The round had mercifully ended, and I could barely see to make my way back to my corner. A torrent of tears streamed from both eyes. "Unlace them," I blurted, thrusting both hands toward Jimmy, my trainer.

"No."

"What do you mean, no? Look at my nose; it's broken."

"Yes, but you are way ahead on points. All you have to do is keep him away from you for one more round, and you're the winner."

I was so hyped on adrenalin I was not thinking rationally, and I took Jimmy's advice. I could look down and see my displaced nose directly under my left eye. Both eyes watered profusely as I answered the bell for the final round and stumbled to the center of the ring. Awaiting my arrival was Bobby Garrigan, a tough Scottish lad fifteen pounds heavier than me and built like the proverbial brick outhouse. We had fought previously and I had always won on points, but I never once put him down or even staggered him.

I must have looked like a rooster jumping around the ring and throwing every punch and kick in my arsenal, not caring whether they landed or not. I just wanted to keep him away so he could not smash my nose again. Mercifully the bell sounded and the fight ended before that happened. I made my way to the nearest phone and called the hospital.

"Hi, this is Dr. Bardsley. Could you please tell me which plastic surgery resident is on call tonight?"

"Dr. Graham is on tonight, Dr Bardsley. Would you like me to page him for you?"

"No, thank you. Who is covering ENT tonight?"

"Dr. Smith is on call until midnight, and then it is Dr. West."

I looked at the clock: nine-thirty. I liked and respected John Smith. In my opinion, Graham was marginally competent. I called Dr. Smith at home and explained the situation. I told him I would go to the emergency department and have an x-ray taken and meet him in the ENT treatment room at eleven o'clock.

I arrived early and waited patiently outside the locked room, tears streaming from both eyes. The treatment room was rarely used at night and was smack in the middle of an extremely long corridor that connected the two major wings of the hospital. John looked exhausted when he arrived. It was Tuesday night, and Wednesday was the busiest day of the week for both of us. Our departments had adjacent operating rooms starting at seven a.m. and running through six in the evening. This meant we residents had to be at the hospital at six a.m. to ensure that the day's surgical patients were ready.

"You're right. The nasal bones are broken," Dr. Smith said as he snapped the x-ray onto the view box. "Have a seat in the treatment chair. This won't take long."

Before I realized it, he began to push a pair of pronged forceps into my nostrils. I grabbed his forearm. "John, what are you doing? What about some local anesthesia?"

"It will only hurt for a moment."

"Anesthesia first!" I said, pointing to my disfigured nose.

He put down the forceps, removed his gloves, and disappeared for what seemed like an extraordinarily long time. I learned later that the cocaine was locked in a room at the far end of the corridor. He had to get the key and then find a nurse to co-sign before he could take it out. He returned with a small glass vile of liquid in one hand and a cotton swab in the other. He swabbed the inside of my nose with the one percent pure cocaine solution and waited five minutes for it to take effect. I knew it would freeze the mucous membrane but have little effect on the bone. *Better than nothing*, I thought.

He slid the tongs into my nose, one fork far up into each nostril, and then he gave a strong quick jerk in an upward and outward motion. Despite preparing myself, the pain was much more intense than I expected. I gave out a loud involuntary shriek.

"There, it's done. Looks perfect." John seemed quite proud of himself. I gingerly felt my nose, and it was certainly lopsided.

"I want to see it. I will be right back"

I hustled down to the nurses' station at the end of the long corridor and asked if there was a mirror. My suspicion was correct; the nose still had a deviation to the left. Back I went to the treatment room where John was getting ready to go home.

"No good. You have to do it again, but please use stronger anesthetic this time."

Several minutes later John returned with two percent cocaine, and we repeated the whole procedure. The pain was worse this time.

Down to the nurses' station I went, then back to the treatment room. "Look at it. It's still crooked." I protested.

John was losing patience with me now. It was after midnight and he was not officially on call anymore, and we both had a very long day ahead of us. I didn't care; my nose was perfectly straight three hours before and I was not going to settle for anything less now. We repeated the whole process two more times until I was satisfied, each time increasing the dosage of the cocaine.

"Do you want a plaster cast or should I pack it with gauze?"

"Neither."

"But you have to have something to stabilize it or it will displace again."

"Thanks, John. I really appreciate everything you have done. Don't worry, I will be very careful."

He did not try to dissuade me as he locked the door behind us, and we went in opposite directions down the long empty corridor.

It was 2:30 in the morning when I unlocked my apartment door. I went straight to my room taking care not to disturb my roommate, Marshal. I removed all the items from the top of my bookshelf, which I had made from boards and red clay bricks. Next I got rid of the pillow and placed two bricks at the end of the bed, leaving enough room for my head to fit in between. I normally slept on my side but this way I could sleep on my back and the bricks, one on each side of my head, would prevent me from rolling over and displacing my fragile nasal bones. I could not stand the thought of wearing a ridiculous looking plaster cast taped to my face or having twenty feet of gauze ribbon jammed up my nose for stabilization.

I was not the least bit tired. The adrenalin was still surging in my body, or so I thought. I turned on the stereo and started doing calisthenics thinking this would make me tired. A few minutes later the door swung open and there stood my bleary eyed roommate, Marshal. I had to turn down the music to hear him.

"DC (he never called me David), what's going on man? Are you high?"

"No, no, not at all. I had my nose broken in the fight tonight, and I have just spent the last two hours at the hospital having it set. I made them do it four times until it was perfect and it hurt like hell despite the cocai…"

Then I realized it was not adrenaline giving me all this energy. For the first time in my life I was high—on cocaine! There would be no sleep for me the rest of that night. I was sitting in the hospital cafeteria at 5:30 a.m. drinking coffee and waiting for rounds to start at 6.

The big crash came three hours later. I felt like every ounce of energy had been sucked out of my body. There was no feeling of nausea, as in an alcohol hangover, but every action both physical and mental took a supreme effort. I hated every moment of that day as I counted the minutes until 6 p.m. when I could go home and sleep. I cannot, to this day, understand why anyone would subject themselves intentionally to this downer, just for the pleasure of four or five hours of alertness and energy. The last thing in the world I needed was something to make me more hyper.

I spent the next forty-two fitful nights, trying to sleep on my back with my head wedged between the two red bricks. My nose healed without incident, or so I thought. During the healing period, I would repeatedly roll my eyes to the left and stare at the outline of my nose to ensure its correctness, and then I would repeat the process by rolling my eyes to the right. Unfortunately this habit became entrenched and to this day, it is a component of my facial tics.

"What are you looking at?" would become a source of continual questioning and embarrassment.

My brother Peter would always ask, "Hey, Dave, is that invisible fly still on the end of your nose?"

The surgery staff and other residents in my department seemed to accept my peculiarities and rarely made mention of them. The spinning and vocalizations had subsided in my teens, but other compulsive behaviors had taken their place. Tying my shoes was and still remains a bit of an arduous task. People are always amazed at the speed at which I can do it. The problem is the degree of tightness is rarely the same, so I have to keep retying them over and over until the right is exactly equal to the left in tightness. This can often take four or five minutes and has frequently caused irritation, especially when I am in a hurry and others are waiting.

CHAPTER TEN
"THE BOOM BENTLEY"

During the last year of my residency, I gave a lot of thought to where I wanted to live and practice. I could have stayed in Halifax, then a city of a quarter of a million people, or gone back to Saint John, where I grew up and where my family still lived, with its population of eighty thousand. In Saint John, I would be the only oral and maxillofacial surgeon and be instantly busy.

I was finally convinced that being a kick-boxer and a surgeon were mutually exclusive. I am a slow learner but I eventually understood that I had to give it up. It had served me well and kept me on an even keel for eight wonderful years, but it was over. This left me with two main passions in my life, skiing and sailing. Both Halifax and Saint John were on the ocean and offered good sailing, but skiing was almost nonexistent in both locations. Besides, I was a small town boy, I wanted a fresh start and the allure of the big city fascinated me.

I graduated in early June and spent the next three months travelling the eastern and western seaboards of Canada and the United States. The only city I looked at in between was Denver,

Colorado. I made a chart with a number of vertical columns. The left-hand column contained the names of all the cities. Each of the other columns was assigned some characteristic that I considered important. Skiing and sailing were the most important columns, but I also included climate, population, traffic, age, demographics etc. Each city received a score from one to ten for each characteristic. When I tallied the numbers, Vancouver, British Columbia, was the winner, and San Francisco was second. Friends laughed at my obsessive behavior when I showed them the chart; they called me a robot. Perhaps they were right.

Surgical residency does not prepare you in any way for the business of running a private practice. The surgical training process takes place in a hospital where everything is handled by the organization. I did not have a clue how to go about setting up a private clinic, nor did I have the money to do so. I wrote to all fourteen oral and maxillofacial surgeons practicing in Vancouver and asked if they were looking for an associate. I received two replies.

As a student I had a great relationship with the bank in Halifax. Over the years they had processed all my government-backed student loans. On my final visit I informed the bank manager I was moving across the country to Vancouver to set up a practice and convinced him to give me a twenty thousand dollar, unsecured loan.

I immediately drove my Volkswagen one thousand miles west to Toronto, sold it, and started shopping for my dream car: a black, 1976, Lincoln town car; the longest car ever made in North America. It was during this search of used car lots (the new Lincolns were much smaller) that I first saw vintage Rolls Royces and Bentleys. They were bigger, blacker, and badder than anything I had ever seen. Most were way out of my price range. The salesman at one lot said he was a collector himself and belonged to the Rolls Royce and Bentley club.

He wrote a name and number on the back of his business card and handed it to me. "Call this gentleman. He is a member of the club and I understand his Bentley might be for sale."

I called and made an appointment to see the car.

Sara answered the door and led me to the living room to meet Jim. He was slouched in a large arm chair and the distinguishing features of his face were obscured by the transparent oxygen mask he was holding over his nose and mouth. When he removed the mask and extended his hand, I was appalled by his ashen appearance.

He removed and replaced the mask every thirty seconds as we conversed. Jim was sixty years old and had been an executive for twenty-five years with a large international paint company. He had been a smoker all his life and six months earlier he suffered a massive heart attack which left him so incapacitated he could no longer work. They were forced to sell their lifelong home because he was unable to climb the four steps leading to the front door, let alone the flight of stairs to the second floor. They had moved into their bungalow three months ago. Jim spent most of his time reading and watching TV. The car was for sale because he could no longer drive or afford it.

"I have been a classic car buff as long as I can remember," he explained. "I have owned and sold eleven different cars during that time, but my dream was always to own an S model Bentley. I had an agent looking in Great Britain for three years before he found this one. It's a 1960 S2 Bentley, bought from an estate; it's always been chauffeur driven, eleven thousand original miles, and I'm the second owner. Would you like to take it for a drive?"

Those were the words I wanted to hear. It took some time for Sara to get Jim mobile, but we eventually made our way to the garage, and when the door opened my mouth dropped. It was magnificent.

"You drive, Dave. I can't."

I opened the door and loaded Jim and his oxygen tank into the passenger seat. As we cruised through the neighborhood he told me about the many ribbons and trophies the Bentley had won in various competitions.

"Are you planning on showing the car?"

I didn't know how to respond, thinking my answer might insult him. "I am not sure at the moment, Jim."

We enjoyed the beautiful drive in silence for a few minutes but I was aware Jim was staring at me, and then he asked "Are you all right?"

How many times had I heard that before? My excitement level was high and as always my facial tics and head jerks were exacerbated. The conversation eventually came around to price.

"Jim, I'm embarrassed to even make an offer. I would love to be able to buy this car but I just finished twelve years in college and the most I could possibly scrape together is fifteen thousand dollars."

A long uneasy silence followed. Finally Jim spoke. "I was expecting to get at least twenty," another long awkward pause, "but you seem like you really appreciate the car and would take care of it. Bring a certified check or bank draft tomorrow, and I will have the papers ready."

I wanted to let out a victory scream, but I fought to keep my composure. When we arrived back at Jim's, I went to help him out of the car. I put my hand on the edge of the window and was about to push the door closed when Jim's hand shot up and grabbed me by the wrist.

"In 1960 this was the best door handle made. There may be better ones today, I don't know, but not in 1960. Never disrespect the car. Never put your hand on the window to close the door. Use the handle."

I apologized profusely, thinking I might have blown the deal.

When I arrived the next day, Jim and Sara were all dressed up. After the money was transferred and the papers signed, Jim asked, "Would you be kind enough to allow us one last ride?"

As we approached the car Jim instructed me to open the trunk; it was filled with trophies and ribbons. My first thought was, *I don't want all this junk.*

"Oh, Jim, I can't take these. They belong to you."

"No, and they don't belong to you either; they belong to the car. If you ever sell it, they go with it."

I opened the back door and helped them in. They talked and reminisced about the old days as I chauffeured them through the neighborhood. Whenever I glanced in the mirror I could see the tears in Jim's eyes and Sara holding his arm tightly. I felt terrible, like I was taking their child. I should have given him the whole twenty thousand.

When we got back to the house, Jim handed me a stack of self-addressed, stamped post cards. "Drop me a note every now and again, and let me know how she is doing. And remember, don't change anything; originality is everything to a collector."

They stood in front of the bungalow waving until I was out of sight.

The next day I started the thousand mile drive home. When I arrived in Halifax I went straight to the biggest car audio store in town. They were shocked at the size of the tubed radio they removed from below the dash; it was the size of a sewing machine. An entirely new sound system was installed with sub woofers so powerful that the license plate vibrated when the base was cranked up. Years later the kids in Vancouver who owned tiny Honda Civics with huge sound systems would name it, *"The Boom Bentley."*

I packed whatever I could into the car, gave the rest to my roommate, and headed west on the four thousand mile trip to Vancouver and my new life. As the years passed, I would come to regret destroying the Bentley's originality. Jim was absolutely right, but I didn't understand that until much later. I had once again given into my compulsive behavior.

CHAPTER ELEVEN
"A FRESH START"

My excitement meter was off the charts the day I rolled into Vancouver. I drove straight into the downtown area of my newly chosen city and parked beside the first phone booth I saw. I only knew one person in Vancouver, my old dental school roommate, Wayne. He knew I would be arriving sometime in the fall but not exactly when. I wanted to surprise him. I knew I could stay with him until I was set up with a job and a place to live. I dropped a quarter into the box, waited anxiously for the tone, and then pushed the buttons.

"Good afternoon, Dr. MacKinnon's office."

"Hi, this is Dr. Bardsley; may I speak to Dr. MacKinnon please?"

"I'm sorry; Dr. MacKinnon is not in the office today. May I help you with something?"

"May I have his home number, please? I'm his old college roommate, and I want to surprise him."

"Oh dear, Dr. MacKinnon left yesterday for Mexico, and he won't be back for three weeks."

My smile evaporated.

The downtown area was filled with large luxury hotels, no place for a poor student. I asked a policeman and he directed me to a moderately priced one. Despite my excitement I slept like I was drugged. I was up at sunrise and by sundown the next day I had rented a small bachelor apartment for a month and rented enough furniture to make it comfortable. The next day I called Drs. Kirby and March, the two surgeons I had spoken to a month before and who might be looking for an associate. I arranged appointments to meet with one on Monday and the other on Tuesday. I made a list of all the other oral and maxillofacial surgeons in the area, bought a city map, and headed out to meet each one.

"Welcome to Vancouver," said Paul Roman, smiling genuinely and extending his hand.

It did not take long to discover we shared a passion: skiing. Paul had a chalet at Whistler which he used every weekend, and he went on a helicopter ski trip each year. We would eventually become good friends.

"We are ready for you, doctor," the nurse said.

"Sorry, Dave; got to go. You are going to love it here in Vancouver. Jane will give you my home number; call me if I can be of any help."

Over the next three days I met the other eleven maxillofacial surgeons. The welcome was anything but warm. The message was the same from each: "You should set up outside the city or in the interior of the province. There are too many surgeons concentrated here; you will starve."

It was not the reception I had imagined, and I felt discouraged. Maybe I should have stayed in Halifax.

Monday morning I drove the forty minutes to the eastern suburb of Westminster to meet with Dr. Kirby. We walked to a Chinese restaurant three blocks from his clinic for lunch. Mike was very businesslike. After sharing some personal information about ourselves, he laid his cards on the table and made me an offer.

"I will give you fifty percent of every dollar you bill and we collect. I will pay all the overhead and staff; you will have no expenses. You work four days straight, have one off, work three more days, then have six off. That way we each work seven days out of every fourteen. What do you think?"

I thought it was a fair arrangement, but my biggest objection was the forty five minute commute. I wanted to live downtown. I was young and single and that was definitely where the action was.

"But remember you will be going in the opposite direction to the traffic. Most commuters will be going from the suburbs into the city center in the morning; you will be doing the opposite."

His point was well taken. I explained I could not give him a decision right away as I had a meeting with Dr. March the next afternoon.

"I just have one more question" he said hesitantly, "Do you have any medical issues I should know about?"

"No, I have no medical problems."

I pumped my fist in the air and cranked up the tunes as I drove back into town in the Boom Bentley. Regardless of what happened tomorrow, I knew I had a job.

I arrived ten minutes early for the four o'clock meeting with Dr. March. The Hyatt's garden lounge was magnificent. It catered to high-end tourists and businessmen. I was neither, and I definitely felt out of place. Hanging over the enormous bar were more martini glasses than I had ever seen in my life. After twelve years of university, I was accustomed only to beer. Cheap beer. At first I was the only patron, but slowly others began to drift in. The very attractive waitress had asked me twice if I would like anything. I declined both times explaining I was waiting for someone. She probably thought some girl had stood me up. I was surprised he hadn't called the lounge with a message saying he was going to be late; perhaps he was stuck in surgery.

"Pardon me. Could you tell me the time please?"

"Six ten, sir. Would you like something else?"

"No, thanks. Just the bill please."

The waitress must have thought I was a pathetic loser, which was exactly how I was feeling. I was digging in my pocket for my credit card when I heard "You must be David."

I looked up and saw a thin man in his late forties with a bulbous nose, short curly hair, beady brown eyes, and an air of confidence. "You look like you are just out of high school," quipped Dr. Marsh.

As we talked I realized I had mistaken his arrogance for confidence. He laid out the conditions of my possible employment as though he was doing me a great favor. All I could think about is how this pompous ass had kept me waiting for more than two hours and had not uttered one word of apology or explanation.

We parted with him saying, "I will talk it over with my partner and let you know."

I did not care that his clinic was only fifteen minutes from where I wanted to live; I rushed home and called Mike Kirby. "I'll take the job."

I spent the first week following Mike around as he did consultations and surgery in his clinic. Next, he introduced me to the staff at the hospital, and I was placed on the *on call* list for the following month. By the end of the first week I felt I was up to speed, so my first patients were booked for the following Monday.

Things went smoothly for the first three days, and I did lots of consultations which resulted in many surgical bookings. My very first patient on the fourth day was a woman in her mid-fifties who was referred because of a blocked salivary duct. She just sat there staring at me, seemingly not paying any attention to my explanation of why the blockage occurred and how I was going to resolve it.

Surely she is being distracted by my blinking or twitching, was my first self-conscious thought. I tried to suppress the tics but as always, this made them worse. Then she caught me completely by surprise.

"Excuse me, Dr. Bardsley, but how long have you been doing surgery?"

I could feel the immediate flush of blood in my face. Panic set in. She would not be filled with confidence to learn that this was my fourth day. I could not lie but my surgical training had started four years ago so I felt justified in saying, "I have been doing surgery for four years. Why do you ask?"

"Well, it's just that you look so young."

"Well, thank you for the compliment, but I can assure you I am much older than I look."

When I finished work that day I went straight to the optometrist in the local mall and purchased a pair of tortoise brown eyeglass frames. No lenses, just the frames. Surely they would make me look older. There was no need to wear them while I was performing surgery as the patients were asleep, but I put then on before every consultation.

This worked well for the first three weeks. Again it was a middle-aged woman who busted me during a consultation. She was completely absorbed in her own thoughts as I explained her impending surgery. Several times she reached toward my face and then, catching herself, retracted her hand. Then it happened.

"Excuse me, Dr. Bardsley. Are there any lenses in those frames?"

"Actually, no, there aren't."

"Then why are you wearing them?"

My brain froze momentarily. "Well, I am aaaahum…I am trying out different frames to see which ones are the most comfortable before they put the lenses in."

"Oh, that's a really good idea."

I hated lying, but I was convinced I was doing it for the patient's peace of mind. Surely they would have more confidence and feel more at ease if they thought I was older and more experienced.

The practice was soon booming. I was booked months ahead, and I loved working seven days out of every fourteen. I had moved to a new apartment in a high-rise, right on the beach. I had met a ton of new people, my bank account was swelling, and life was very good.

"Pick Me"

"Dave, I have the perfect car for you. I sold it to a client five weeks ago and he was just transferred to Hong Kong."

I was standing butt-naked in the locker room of The Parc. I had met John the day I joined the health club. He ran a very successful exotic car business and I had run into him on numerous social occasions.

"I don't think I need another car, John. The Boom Bentley is working just fine."

"Why don't I bring it by your place tonight, just for fun? I won't tell you what it is; I want it to be a surprise."

Six hours later I was standing in front of my apartment building drooling over a midnight black Porsche 928 turbo, gleaming under the street lights. John handed me the keys and said, "Let's take it for a spin."

Minutes later we were cruising down Bidwell Street, gliding past the lovely young hookers displaying their goods on every corner. Vancouver was famous for them. They all waved and beckoned us to pull over. We stopped at the traffic light at the corner of Sixth, and a particularly beautiful young girl ran towards the car and threw herself spread eagle on the hood yelling, "Pick me! Pick me!"

There was no denying it; the car had sex appeal. It turned every head as we cruised through the downtown core. Twenty minutes later we pulled into the driveway of my building.

"What's wrong, don't you like it? You haven't even tried it on the highway yet," protested John.

I got out and closed the door, making sure I used the handle. "Come by the clinic tomorrow with the car and the papers. My accountant Mary will have a check waiting for you."

Life just got a whole lot better, or so I thought.

Despite the new Porsche and the fact I was going against the traffic, I still regretted the daily forty-five minute commute to work each way. My logical hemisphere reasoned that if I worked eight hours a day and slept eight hours, I was left with eight hours for me. An hour and a half commute, represented eighteen percent of my free time.

After ten months I gave Mike my notice. I would leave in two months to set up my own practice downtown. It turned out to be one of the best decisions I ever made. Once I started looking, it did not take me long to find a suitable space and start preparing my clinic. It was exactly one block from Dr. March and his partner. They didn't exactly welcome me to the neighborhood.

I received dozens of applications for the clinic jobs. I soon had a crackerjack staff and we were up and running. I was surprised how quickly the practice grew. The staff was incredible; my success was their success. I was one cog in a well oiled machine. Although their salaries were very generous, that is not what motivated them.

Years later I allowed them to set their own salaries. A job well done is its own satisfaction, but what is much more gratifying is when it is recognized by others. No matter how hectic or busy the day was, I never left the clinic without individually thanking each of the staff for their wonderful effort. I truly appreciated them and I was not afraid to tell them.

My father had always told me, "David, everyone is smarter than you about something. If it is in your power, give them a chance to show it and they will be loyal forever."

"*My Friend Ian*"

I jumped out of the shower still dripping and grabbed the phone on the sixth ring

"Dave, this is Wayne. I am having a few people over to my place Saturday night before we go out. Ian Bruce will be there; he says he knows you from the kickboxing club in Halifax."

"Can't say I remember him, but I will see you Saturday."

I could not recall any Ian Bruce, but the club was large and because I was a black belt, I was known to many of the novice students. I was not in the door at Wayne's fifteen seconds when he stepped towards me with an outstretched hand.

"Hi, Dave. Remember me? I'm Ian Bruce?"

I recognized that shy grin instantly. Five years before I was paired off with Ian to practice a series of non-contact moves which culminated in him throwing a punch to the side of my head. He was supposed to pull the punch at the last moment. He did not. Twice he landed a cracking left fist to the side of my head, and twice he apologized profusely, with that shy grin on his face. Ian was a mid level student then, and I know he enjoyed thumping a black belt. I did not know his name at the time.

Now, five years later, on the opposite side of the country, we meet again.

"Where are you living, Dave?"

"On the seventeenth floor of the building next door. Apartment 1701. I think I have the best view in all of Vancouver. I'm on the water's edge overlooking the harbor and it's truly magnificent. How about you Ian, are you living in the downtown area?"

"Yep. I also have a magnificent view. In fact it might be slightly better than yours."

"Impossible! There is no building closer to the water's edge than mine."

"Yes, I know. I live in the same building, one floor above you, apartment 1801. We're neighbors."

Ian, Wayne and I would become the Three Amigos. We did everything together: skied in the winter, sailed in the summer, trained in the gym together, partied hard and often. Our professions insured we had plenty of money and free time to enjoy it. We were young, single, and in the prime of our lives; invincible we thought.

Our friendship would remain for the next twenty-eight years. We shared many incredible adventures, but it would come to a heartbreaking end. I did not know it at the time but Ian's tragic death would change the course of my life.

CHAPTER TWELVE
"YOU STUTTER, I TWICH"

My surgery clinic had been open less than a year when Jane, one of my nurses said,

"You know, Dr. Bardsley, just before the patients see you for their consultation, I think it would be very helpful if they could see a video explaining their impending procedure and what they might expect post-operatively. It would save you time, and the patients would be much more knowledgeable and would have more time to think about what questions they would like to ask you during the consultation."

I thought it was a splendid idea.

Every patient was referred so we knew exactly why they were coming. We chose two of the most common surgical procedures and started scouring the professional literature to see if such videos existed. They did not, so I decided to make one.

One of my nurses had a friend whose son, Jason, had just graduated from a film production school. I met with Jason, and we decided the project was feasible. There were to be four videos in total: a pre-operative and post-operative video for the two most common surgical procedures I performed. I wrote out all the information I wanted to convey, and Jason helped put it into script form. We hired two actors to play the patients: Bob, 20, who had just finished acting school, and Madeline, a 68-year-old veteran of the local stage.

The videos were to be shot in the clinic on two successive weekends. Jason explained that multiple takes are costly, so we all memorized our lines well in advance. Things went smoothly the first weekend, and Jason seemed pleased. He spent the next three days editing and adding the music and the animation shots. He called on Thursday.

"Hi, Dave. I have the final product ready for your review. I will drop it off at the clinic this afternoon, and I would appreciate it if you would look at it tonight and call me at home and let me know if you want to make any changes before this weekend's shoot."

He dropped it off around two that afternoon and I was happy when the final patient scheduled that day called at the last moment and cancelled. I shot down to my car and raced home. I think at some point everyone fantasizes about being a movie star. Perhaps I was destined to be the next Jack Nicholson.

I burst through my apartment door, threw my briefcase on the couch, pulled the curtains tight, and popped in the video. The title burst onto the screen, and the music started.

Wow, this was the big time! In the opening shot my whole torso was visible above the desk where I was seated, but as I started talking, the camera zoomed in until my face filled the entire screen. This was before the age of digital photography, and although I had seen myself many times in still photographs, this was the first time on video.

I lack the ability to adequately describe the anguish and humiliation I felt as I watched in utter shame. I looked like I was being electrocuted. The blinking and twitching facial muscles were ten times worse than I had ever imagined. I fought to hold back the tears.

My God, is this what other people see when they look at me?

I watched it several times from start to finish, hoping that each time it would somehow miraculously improve. I stared, much like you stare at a person with severe burns, even though you try not to. It took over an hour to regain my composure and find the courage to call Jason.

"I just watched it. My God, it will frighten the patients before they see me. I don't care what it costs; we are going to do it over again. Jason, please, you have to tell me when the blinking and twitching are too pronounced, and we will shoot the scene again."

There was a long silence followed by, "I agree."

I studied it over and over and marked the scenes that had to be redone. We had three very long days the following weekend but we were able to reshoot what was needed and shoot the next two videos as well.

I do not see myself blinking, twitching or head jerking when I look in the mirror but the constant questions never let me forget that this is part of who I am.

"Do you have something in your eye?"
"What's wrong with your neck?"
"Are you all right?"

I just had no idea it was so pronounced and so obvious. Despite being brutally painful, in the end the experience was probably a good thing. At least now the patients would not be as shocked as they might have been witnessing my strangeness for the first time during the consultation. Perhaps that was the real reason my nurse suggested the videos in the first place.

"Run Rod Run"

"Damn it! What's your problem anyway?" protested Rod.

"Piss off, faggots," muttered the lumbering hulk, as he stumbled to the back corner where his snickering buddies waited.

"That's the third time that jerk intentionally bumped into me and spilled my drink," protested Rod.

"They're getting more drunk and aggressive by the minute; I better find my sister," exclaimed Rita.

Rod attended law school in Canada and then studied tax law at Harvard. He had moved to Vancouver the year before and headed the tax department of a large downtown law firm. He was several inches shorter than me and although he was not the least overweight, he had a round boyish face with soft features atop which sat the world's most perfect hair. Each uniformly bleached blond strand was cut to its ideal length and remained in its designated position regardless of whatever forces of man or nature tried to make it otherwise. He was definitely good looking, but not in a ruggedly handsome sort of way. I had met Rod through my friend Wayne six months previously. We had a great deal in common and instantly became good friends.

The intercom squawked. "Dr. Bardsley, your friend Rod is on line two."

"Thanks, Merna."

"Hey Rod, what's up?"

"Our lucky day my friend. Do you remember Rita Stephens and her four sisters?"

"I sure do. They're all gorgeous, especially the two married ones."

"Well, Rita just called and invited us to a party at her sister's place on Saturday night. It's on Sudbury St. Do you know where that is?"

"Yes, it's over on the east side. That's a pretty rough section of town."

"Who cares? All five of the sisters will be there."

"Ok. Let's take one car; I'll pick you up at eight thirty."

We arrived around nine and as I had expected, it was in a tough neighborhood. We decided to park my Porsche several blocks away, fearing it might be vandalized by drunks leaving the party.

The rambling old house was situated on a poorly lit corner, but the noise coming from within confirmed we were at the right place. We descended several steps and tried to enter through what appeared to be a sub-basement door. It was locked; and our repeated poundings could not be heard above the blaring music.

"This entrance doesn't look like it's ever used," I said. "The main entrance must be on the other side. Let's go around."

We found the front door on the opposite side of the house. It was wide open so we followed the music into a kitchen. It was empty except for a couple loading bags of ice into the freezer.

"Hi, I'm David, and this is Rod; we're friends of Rita. Has she arrived yet?"

"Everyone is in the basement; the stairs are at the end of that hall."

Rod opened the door and the music volume instantly tripled. We started down the stairs but the dim lighting bouncing off the twirling disco ball made vision difficult for a few seconds, until our eyes adjusted.

Half way down Rod stopped abruptly, looked back up at me and said. "It's all guys; let's get out of here."

"Wait!" I said "Let's see if Rita is here first, then we'll go."

Fifteen to eighteen guys had congregated around the base of the stairs. They were yelling to be heard above the music and most seemed to know each other. The basement was at least forty feet long, with two small sub-basement windows on the adjacent wall. Between the windows were three enormous posters at least seven feet tall of Mick Jagger flanked by Queen and the Beatles.

At the far end were about twenty-five girls, all dressed in their finest party outfits. My mind instantly shot back to those awkward school dances that I usually tried to avoid. The girls congregated at one end, the boys at the other. Rita spotted us right away and came running over. She led us back and introduced us to every girl. We were in heaven. Over the next hour more people arrived but the polarity remained unchanged. Guys at one end;

Rod, me, and the girls at the other. They surrounded us, and we did our best to keep them entertained.

Rita explained that she did not know many of the guys. Some were construction workers but most were commercial fishermen. You did not need much of an education to make a lot of money in the herring roe business in those days. The entire catch went to the Japanese sushi market, at exorbitant prices. The season was only six weeks long, three in the spring and three in the fall. In some areas fishing would only be permitted for a frantic six hours. The boats would jostle so close their nets and gear would tangle, tempers would flair, and shots would be fired. The Coast Guard and Fisheries Department were often unable to prevent deaths from gunshots. The payout, however, was enormous. Unskilled deckhands could earn in excess of one hundred and fifty thousand dollars, for just six weeks work. They would collect unemployment for the other forty-five weeks. Drugs and nonstop partying were a way of life ashore.

We had the attention of all the girls, and the fishermen hated us. Rod and I had been accused of being gay in the past; but never by women. Apparently, if you were reasonably attractive, showered daily, wore nice clothes, spoke in complete sentences, and cleaned your fingernails on a regular basis you were gay. Our Versace clothes and Rod's perfect hair and pink sweater did not help matters, nor did people constantly mistaking my blinking as winking. They decided we must be gay, and the bashing was about to begin.

Rita returned with her sister, Sheri, who lived in the house.

"I'm so sorry," said Sheri. "I don't know what is wrong with those idiots. I tried talking to them but they are too drunk and all they want to do is fight you two. Don't try to make it up the stairs, you are safer here. I'll call the police right now. Stay here."

Several of the guys crossed the floor and verbally threatened us. The girls intervened and started yelling, telling them how stupid and immature they were acting, but it only made them more macho.

All the kickboxing skills in the world would not help me now. There were twenty of them and two of us. Sheri returned shortly with the bad news.

"The police are on their way but its Saturday night and they're swamped; they'll be here in an hour or so."

A half dozen of the fishermen began pointing at us and then started punching their open hands with their fists. They started moving towards us as a group. There was no escape. The only stairs were behind them.

"I can't believe this is happening," uttered Rod. "Don't they know I am a lawyer? They will all go to jail, and I'll sue them."

"Protect your eyes and face, Rod. Don't let them get you on the floor or they'll start kicking!"

"Bang, Bang, Bang!" The noise was clearly audible above the music.

Gunshots! was my first thought. Then I heard it again.

Bang, Bang!

The fishermen heard it, too. Everyone froze and turned toward the giant posters on the wall. Mick Jagger started to shake violently. Suddenly the poster ripped and the previously concealed door behind it flung open. A tall bewildered figure stumbled through, immediately followed by four or five of his equally large companions. They were as startled by their abrupt entrance as we were.

"It's Julio, from the gym." I blurted and immediately ran toward him. "Hey Julio, it's me, David, from the gym. Remember me?"

"Oh ya, h-h-hey man, w-w-w-what are you doing in my neighborhood?"

"Are these your friends, behind you?"

"Ya, this is Larrie, B-b-ben, Angello…"

They were all quite drunk but I didn't care; they were big and there were six of them. I quickly waved Rod over as Julio continued to introduce his friends.

"Julio, the beer is upstairs in the kitchen." I pointed to the stairs behind the fisherman. "You go first."

Julio and my newfound wall of friends started to move toward the fishermen and the stairs behind them.

"Rod, let's bolt," I pointed to our newly opened escape route. Neither the fisherman nor Julio and his friends saw us flee. Once outside we sprinted the three blocks to my Porsche without pausing to look over our shoulder.

I had seen Julio several times at The Parc, a downtown health club where we both were members. I knew his name but nothing more. The club attracted an incredible collection of characters. Most were promoters and lawyers from the notorious Vancouver Stock Exchange. A month after I joined, an investigative report by a national television network had exposed enormous fraud on the Exchange. Seventy percent of the listed companies were frauds. Still the Exchange flourished.

Despite their crooked dealings, the promoters were a likable lot. My favorite was Jimmy "The Salt." He had blown off half his foot with a shotgun shell full of gold dust. Gold stock promoters frequently shot gold dust (salting) into the ground of a mining lease. They would then take prospective investors to the site and let them accidently discover the gold.

The club manager, Tommy, had spent two years in prison for loan sharking. He was audio taped threatening to break the knees of a "client" who owed him money. Brandon had done time for killing his wife's lover after he caught the two of them in bed. The club was owned and frequented by the Netti family; one of the oldest, wealthiest, and most respected families in the province. Both father and son had served in the highest political office, Premier of British Columbia. Lawyers, politicians, business executives, and crooks. It was hard to distinguish one from the other—the perfect place for a blinking, twitching, head jerking surgeon to fit in. I found it fascinating.

The following Tuesday I arrived at the club later than usual, and my normal workout partner, Wayne, was just finishing. I changed and went straight down to the weight room. Julio and his friend Mike were hard at it.

"H-h-hey man, how you doing? That was a great p-p-party on Saturday, wasn't it? How come you left s-s-so early?" asked Julio.

"It's a long story buddy." I replied, "I'll tell you about it sometime but for now, thanks."

Several weeks later we were sitting in the steam room together. "Hey D-d-d-d-dave, I guess you noticed that I s-s-s-stutter sometimes?" He then went on to explain he has had the affliction all his life. He had tried therapy as recently as three years before. One of the exercises was getting on a bus, sitting beside a stranger, introducing himself, and then starting a conversation. "It's much worse when I'm excited or n-n-nervous," he explained.

"You know, Julio, I think I stutter too. I don't do it with words; I do it with my face. I'm sure you noticed my tics, twitches, and head jerks. I have had them all my life and they get much worse when I am excited or nervous. You stutter, and I twitch. What's the difference, really?"

From that day on our friendship blossomed. It went from the occasional gym workout together, to being partners in a ski chalet at Whistler for ten years. Over the decades we have shared vacations and adventures far too numerous to count. Thirty years later, we remain the very closest of friends. Despite living in different parts of the country, we see each other often, and it is always the very best of times.

CHAPTER THIRTEEN
"WHAT SMELL?"

I stepped up to the door and was about to push the buzzer but the party sounds coming from within were so loud I knew no one would hear it. I pushed the door open and strode in trying my best to exude an air of confidence.

"God, what is that smell?" I heard someone mutter from the couch to my right. Janet, the hostess, spotted me right away and was by my side in an instant.

"Hi, David." She paused. "What is that smell? Is that you?"

I looked down at my feet expecting to see dog poop on my shoes. I smelled nothing.

"Did you take a bath in cologne?"

By now everyone within twenty feet had stopped talking and was staring at me. "Well, I did put on a little after shave, yes."

"You must have bathed in it! Come with me."

Janet grabbed my arm and whisked me through the living room so fast I barely had time to nod to the few people I recognized. My face was flushed with embarrassment and my twitching intensified.

She closed the door to the bathroom behind us. "There are towels on the shelf. Take a quick shower and get rid of that smell; it's overpowering. I'll see you in a few minutes."

Following a thorough scrubbing, I made my second entrance into the party, this time with considerably less confidence. It took years before my friends finally stopped niggling me about the incident.

Six months before that party I had helped Janet out of a difficult situation. In appreciation she gave me a lovely gift basket of grooming items which included a bottle of aftershave lotion. I had never used aftershave; in fact, I had such little facial hair I only shaved once a week. I promptly put the aftershave under my bathroom sink and forgot about it. Three days before the party I was having my apartment painted, and the painters asked me to remove everything from underneath the sink so they could paint the inside of the cabinet.

That evening, I showered before getting dressed for the party and it was time for my weekly shave. When I finished, I set the razor back down on the countertop with all the items I had not yet put back under the sink. It was then I noticed the bottle of aftershave, and I thought, *What the heck?*

I opened the bottle and poured some of the mysterious green liquid into my cupped hand, which I immediately held up to my nose, but only a very faint scent was discernable. I slopped it on my face and neck and when finished was surprised that I didn't smell anything. I remembered seeing an advertisement for fragrance on TV many years before to place perfume or cologne on any area of the body one would like kissed. Since I did not notice any odor whatsoever, I poured out an even larger handful and proceeded to rub it over my entire body. Detecting a faint pleasant odor, I got dressed and confidently headed for the party.

The day following the party, the paint was finally dry, and I started putting all the items back under the sink where they belonged. I opened the bottle of aftershave, smelled the mysterious green liquid that had so offended everyone the night before and detected almost no odor. I had long since grown accustomed to people staring at me; my tics, twitches, and head jerks were not under my control but the aftershave was so I promptly threw it in the garbage.

"*Clinic Fire*"

What's going on?

I leaned as far out over the balcony railing as I could to get a better view along the side of the building.

What? The fire engines are stopping in front of this building!

I turned and slid the glass door open. The smoke in the clinic hallway was readily visible. I ran past the three operating rooms and reception area to the recovery room at the end of the long hallway. I was met by a startled Mrs. Walker standing in the doorway; she immediately spit the blood soaked gauze bandages out of her mouth and yelled, "It's a fire, isn't it?"

Mrs. Walker had been the last patient of the day. She had recovered nicely from her surgery and the general anesthetic. The nurse would bring whoever was coming to take the patient home into the recovery room and go over the post-operative instructions with both of them, as the patients themselves frequently had little or no memory of the entire event.

The single most frequent post-operative complication we dealt with was a vaso-vagal attack, better known as a faint. It was rarely the patient who fainted; it was usually the person who came to take them home. In this case it was Tina, Mrs. Walker's daughter. When Tina entered the recovery room, she took one look at her mother and promptly fainted. Fifteen minutes and numerous cold compresses later she claimed she was perfectly fine. She stood up, adjusted her disheveled clothes and promptly collapsed in a heap on the floor again. She repeated the entire scenario two more times. Except for the nurse Linda and me, the entire staff had long since departed.

"Linda, there is no sense in both of us being here. You go home; I'll wait here until Tina is able to drive her mother."

Linda left and twenty minutes later I heard the fire engines. With Tina and her mother still in the recovery room, I went out onto the balcony to see if I could tell where they were going.

"Don't panic, Mrs. Walker. It's just a little smoke but we are going to evacuate just to be safe."

My adrenaline was surging but I tried not to show it. I could feel my tics escalating as I pulled Tina off the stretcher and threw her over my shoulder in a dead-man-lift. I grabbed Mrs. Walker by the arm and headed for the front door of the clinic. Moments later we were in the fourth floor lobby. I pointed to the door in the corner.

"No, not the elevator. We have to take the stairs."

Despite just having oral surgery and a general anesthetic, Mrs. Walker navigated the stairs remarkably well. Tina was another story. She was draped over my shoulder with the full weight of her body born by her stomach. As we bounced down the stairs, she became nauseated and threw up all over my back. Her stiletto shoes fell off on the second landing. We hustled down the four flights of stairs and with ten more steps to go, the door at the bottom of the stairwell burst open and three firemen in full gear rushed in.

"Do you need any help?"

"We're ok now, but I think there are still people on the third floor."

They nearly knocked us over as they rushed upward carrying all their gear. The last fireman stopped, turned around, put his hand on my shoulder and said, "Are you sure you're ok buddy?"

I knew my twitching and grimacing must be out of control. "I'm fine."

We made our way across the street from the building and I sat Tina and her mother on a lawn as we watched more fire trucks arrive. The response seemed disproportionately large, but I later learned the fire department knew the medical-dental building had large stores of oxygen and other explosive anesthetic gases. Tina was now fully alert. I walked her and Mrs. Walker to their car which was at the end of the block and I insisted on driving them home.

I took a cab back to the clinic expecting to see the building in rubbles. It was not. The fire on the second floor had been minimal, although it did produce considerable smoke which disseminated throughout the building. The same firemen we had met in the stairwell accompanied me back up the stairs to my clinic. I collected Tina's shoes along the way. He suggested I go to emergency.

"You know, Doc; they taught us in fire training that sometimes even a little smoke inhalation can cause problems with the nervous system. I think you really should get checked out." He was too embarrassed to say any more.

"Thanks but I'll be fine."

He instructed me to leave the windows and sliding doors open all weekend, which I did. By the time we reopened in three days, there was barely a hint of smoke.

Mrs. Walker called four days later. "I just wanted to call and thank Dr. Bardsley and the whole staff for the wonderful care I received. My healing is progressing much faster and much easier than I expected. You are going to think I am crazy for asking this, but my daughter can't find her shoes. I don't suppose by some chance she left them at your clinic when she came to pick me up?"

No mention was ever made of the fire ordeal. Anesthesia and amnesia are a wonderful combination.

"I can't understand why you didn't smell the smoke," said Dr. John Roberts, an ear nose and throat surgeon. It was two weeks later and I had just finished entertaining my colleagues in the surgeons' lounge at Lions Gate Hospital with the story. "Do you have an olfactory problem?"

I made some lame joke about my only olfactory problem was how bad my socks smelled after I exercised. It did however start me thinking. Why indeed did I not smell the smoke or for that matter the aftershave, when I overdosed on it? Several days later, I called John's office and made an appointment to see him.

"Do you have a history of sinus infections?" he asked.

"No."

"Mumps or measles?"

"No."

"Any nasal trauma?"

"What do you mean?"

"Have you ever broken your nose?"

How could I have been so stupid? Of course! If only my head jerking had kicked in at the right moment I might have avoided Bobby Garrigan's crashing right fist in the third round of our kickboxing match. The fracture must have extended past the nasal bones and into the cribriform plate where it damaged my olfactory nerve. John performed some simple tests and determined I had lost eighty percent of my sense of smell. I never realized anything was wrong all those years because I could smell a little; it was just not nearly as intense for me as for most people. Suddenly everything made sense.

On the bright side, I am never tempted by the delicious aroma of unhealthy foods. Proper nutrition takes no willpower on my part. Thanks Bobby. To this day I never take a chance with cologne or aftershave and I am extremely cautious around gas stoves and barbecues.

CHAPTER FOURTEEN
"THE BIG SHOCK"

"David, you are on the staff at the children's hospital in Vancouver, aren't you?" asked Mary, my sister-in-law.

"Yes, I am."

"Well, I think Michael Junior has Tourette syndrome. There is no one here experienced with the disorder and the pediatrician suggested we take him to Halifax. I was hoping you could have him evaluated when he comes to visit you to go skiing at the end of the month."

"I'm sure I can arrange it."

I had some vague idea that Tourette syndrome (TS) was a mild form of autism. I must have been absent from school the day they taught us about it.

I met my nephew Mike, then twelve, and his eleven-year-old brother Pat at the airport the following Thursday. Mike's appointment was for ten o'clock the next morning and we were headed up to Whistler to ski immediately afterwards. We arrived for the appointment 15 minutes early but Dr. Miller was able to see us right away. The diagnosis of TS starts with a few simple blood tests to rule out certain organic conditions that can cause similar symptoms. Once this is done, the entire diagnosis is based on a history of past and present behavior.

Mike waited outside while Dr. Miller asked me a series of questions and then asked Mike to come in. He sat directly in front of the psychiatrist's desk and Dr. Miller sat opposite him holding a clipboard. I sat over in the corner so I would not be a distraction. Dr. Miller had a litany of questions. Did he make strange uncontrollable noises? Did he spin, flap his arms, or stamp his feet uncontrollably? Was he aware of any blinking, twitching, or head jerking? Was there any need to balance things evenly or ensure his shoelaces were of equal tightness? Most of his questions Mike answered in one word responses, always in the negative.

"No; not really. No. No. I don't think so! No. Never."

In sharp contrast, I sat in the corner silently answering all the same questions as they pertained to me and my childhood. My answers were polar opposites. *"Yes. Yes. I think so. Yes. Always."*

I was astounded at the realization unfolding in front of me. *My God, I have Tourette syndrome.*

When the evaluation was over Dr. Miller explained, "Mike has a few facial tics which will probably disappear as he grows older, but he definitely does not have Tourette's and it is unlikely he would ever develop it at his age. Is there anything else you would like to ask before we finish up?"

My response was immediate, "Yes there is. Can I make an appointment to see you next week?"

"I don't understand. I just told you he does not have Tourette's."

"No, the appointment is for me. I answered yes to almost every question you asked Mike. I am sure I have it."

"Dave, this is a children's hospital."

"I know, but please; I need to speak to someone in confidence."

I read everything I could find on the subject and my mind conjured up a series of possible negative consequences. Ten days later, Dr. Miller confirmed the diagnosis. I had the Tourette Triad; TS, ADHD, and OCD.

"I am going to ask that you keep this completely confidential. I don't want any record of your diagnosis to exist."

"I am not sure I understand."

"I wouldn't want the licensing board to know about it and if I were ever involved in a malpractice suit it might be an issue; I'm not sure and I don't want to find out." I asked Dr. Miller for his notes and when I got home I destroyed them.

He suggested that one of the neuroleptic drugs might be a good choice in controlling my symptoms, but I knew there was no cure. Facial tics and uncontrollable muscle twitching are usually the first signs. Many sufferers have uncontrolled head jerking, spastic torso jerks, flapping of the arms, and foot stamping. Other types of concurrent compulsive behaviors are very prevalent. The symptoms vary widely. Fifty percent also have attention deficit, hyperactivity, and obsessive compulsive disorder. Vocalizations must be present for the diagnosis of TS to be made. This can be as mild as persistent throat clearing all the way to uncontrolled outbursts of various sounds or entire words. The most publicized is corprolalia, the uncontrolled blurting of profanities, frequently at the most socially inopportune time. Then the sufferer continues speaking often without realizing anything abnormal has occurred.

Finally, it all made sense. I fit the pattern perfectly. My involuntary facial tics; twitching and grimaces; the head jerks; the blurting and elongation of the letter nnnnnn; the spinning; my hyperactivity; and my attention deficit. How could thirty-two years have passed without someone making the diagnosis or at least suggesting the problem might be TS? I am sure my medical colleagues must have suspected it all along but were too embarrassed to enquire. Most of all, I was angry with myself. It was such an enormous part of my life. Why did I not discover it sooner?

Once the initial shock was over, there was a comforting relief knowing that my lifelong peculiarity had a name and I was not unique or alone. Two hundred thousand people in the United States alone suffer from Tourette syndrome. The hardest part was accepting I will have it all my life, and there is nothing I can do about it. I felt ashamed and kept my secret for many years.

Two weeks later as I was leaving the hospital I decided to pop into the medical library and do some research on the drug Dr. Miller had suggested. Like all psychotropic medications, neuroleptics cross the blood brain barrier and affect how we think, how we feel, and ultimately how we behave; basically the very core of who we are.

The manufacturer stated, "The three most common side effects of all neuroleptics are weight gain, sedation, and cognitive dulling."

I knew what cognitive dulling meant but I saw a dictionary on the adjacent table so just for fun I decided to look it up. I found the word *cognitive* and the word *dulling* but I could not find the phrase *cognitive dulling*. Puzzled, I searched a second and third dictionary and still could not find it. Then I looked up the word *stupidity*. All three dictionaries defined *stupidity* as *cognitive dulling*.

The following day I called one of the manufactures, told them who I was, and said I had some questions about their drug. The polite receptionist transferred me to the public relations department who quickly passed me to a second, third, and fourth department. Finally a chirpy young man who identified himself as Ted was ready to answer my questions.

"Ted, this is Dr Bardsley. I am considering taking one of your neuroleptic drugs and I see your literature reports one of the side effects is stupidity, is that right?"

"No doctor, that is completely incorrect"

"Well I have it right in front of me and it says, quote, *"Weight gain, sedation, and cognitive dulling."*

"Cognitive dulling, yes; but that's not stupidity."

"Well Ted, I suggest you contact the Oxford, Webster and American Collegiate dictionaries and straighten them out because all three of them are defining *stupidity* as "*cognitive dulling.*"

No response.

"So Ted, here are my two questions: is this stupidity dose dependent? If I double the amount of the drug will my stupidity double?"

More silence.

"My second question is: what will happen to my stupidity when I stop taking the drug? Will it go away? Will half of it go away, or none of it?"

A long pause ensued before Ted responded. "I am sorry Dr. Bardsley, I am going to defer this to our research department and they will be in contact with you."

That was the last I heard from them.

Whoever said, *"It is not what happens to you in life that matters; it is how you deal with it,"* must have had Tourette's.

"A Friend Is Gone"

I grabbed the phone on the first ring thinking it was Wendy. It was Sunday night and we had plans to see a movie.

"Dave, its Paul Read. I have some good and bad news for you buddy. One of our heli-ski group, Gerry Lavigne, had a ruptured appendix removed two days ago. That's the bad news. He is doing fine and went home yesterday, but he won't be able to go on the heli-ski trip to the Bugaboos next week. That's the good news; at least for you. We all booked and paid for the trip a year ago and there are no refunds at this late date. I immediately thought of you. You always talked about joining us if the opportunity ever arose. It gets better; Gerry is going to lose his money anyway so he is trying to sell his package for half price. It's a once-in-a-lifetime chance, Dave."

"Paul, I would love to. I am drooling already. I'll get the staff on it first thing tomorrow and see if we can shift the surgeries. I'm on call at the hospital, but I am sure I can switch with someone. I'll call you tomorrow night."

I called Wendy and suggested we go for a run instead of the movie. I was much too excited to sit still. She did not share my exuberance. I fidgeted like a six-year-old for more than two hours, unable to concentrate on the screen in front of me and it was not my ADHD; it was pure anticipation and excitement.

The patients who had been booked for consultations were the easiest to reschedule. We could accommodate most of the clinic surgeries by adding an additional operating day the coming week. We would work five days that week instead of the usual four, and luckily an anesthesiologist was available. Things looked promising; then came the snag.

Every third Wednesday I had an operating room in the hospital for the entire day. Canada's socialist medical system works very well if they scrape you off the street and throw you in an ambulance and whisk you to emergency. Otherwise you wait and wait and wait. The patients who were booked for the hospital the following Wednesday had been waiting a minimum of five months for their surgical date. As strong as the desire to go heli-skiing burned inside me, I just could not in good conscience cancel those hospital patients and make them wait several more months. I called Paul that night and explained. We were both bitterly disappointed.

"Don't worry, my friend. We will make it happen another time. Meanwhile, I will make some sweet turns in that waist-deep champagne powder just for you."

"Make sure you take lots of pictures. We'll look at them over a beer when you get back."

Eight days later I put my gym bag down at the front door and fumbled as my head jerks made inserting the key difficult. I could hear the phone ringing, but I knew there was no sense hurrying as the caller would hang up before I could reach it. To my surprise they did not hang up. It must have rung fifteen times before I got to it.

"Hell, David. Where have you been? I have been trying to reach you for two hours."

It was, Bill. "I was at the gym. What's up?"

"Janet called several hours ago. Paul is dead."

A long period of silence followed. "What do you mean? He's up in the Bugaboos skiing."

"He was killed in an avalanche this morning, along with three others. You know two of them."

It took almost a week to locate the bodies and send them home. The helicopter normally held ten skiers. Their group had nine. I would have been the tenth. I lost the battle to hold back the tears as I realized Paul and I would have been skiing side-by-side, matching each other turn for turn, as we did most weekends at Whistler. Our time together was always spent pursuing our common passion. It was pure joy. Had my conscience not kept me from canceling those surgeries I may well have suffered the same fate.

Paul may have asked others about me. I will never know. But he never once asked me if I had a problem, was there something wrong with me, or why I blinked or jerked my head back and forth. He accepted me the way I was. Few people did.

CHAPTER FIFTEEN
"BIG RED"

"Hi, David. Who's your friend?"

I could barely hear her question over the pounding disco music. "Oh. Hi, Lucy. Nice to see you. This is Brian."

"I'm sitting at a table in the back of the club with my friend Deborah. Why don't you two join us?"

"Thanks, we just got here so I think we'll get a drink first and we'll join you later on."

Brian was a physician who went to the same health club as I did. The Parc was located two floors below, in the same building as the disco. It was Friday night around ten o'clock and we had just finished a late workout. At Brian's suggestion we had walked up the two flights of stairs to Sneaky Pete's nightclub. Many of my friends frequented the place, partly because of the location above the health club and partly because we knew the owner, Pete. Like most night clubs, it was dimly lit, but we had positioned ourselves beside the dance floor where the light was better and all the action was taking place.

After a while, Brian said, "Why don't we go to the back and find Lucy and her friend?"

"Use your head, Brian. If Lucy and her friend are hanging out in the dim corner of the club it's probably because her friend is shy or not very attractive, or probably both. Go ahead if you are interested in Lucy, but I am not interested in meeting her friend."

We stood there for awhile, more mesmerized by the light bouncing off the disco ball than by the couples throwing down their best moves on the dance floor. Donna Summer blared through the sound system. Disco was king and I loved the music. Standing beside me was a short, rather fleshy brunette with a tense expression on her face.

"Would you like to dance?" she mumbled.

"Sorry, what was that?"

"I said, would you like to dance?"

I felt bad I hadn't heard her the first time and had made her ask twice; she must have thought I was a bit of a jerk. I tried to lessen the tension with a little humor. "God, I thought you'd never ask! Let's go."

She wasn't a great dancer and neither was I, but I didn't care. I loved to dance. I was having a great time and it showed. After three or four songs, I asked if she wanted to sit down.

"Not unless you do."

Perfect. I was really getting into the music and I was very aware that most of the people were watching me. I whirled and twirled and strutted. My childhood spinning served me well on the dance floor. A short time later I noticed that many of the dancers were looking away from me and were fixated on the other side of the crowded floor. I maneuvered my partner in that direction, until I saw what drew their attention.

It was a tall, drop-dead-gorgeous redhead who danced like she was in a music video. We caught each other's eye immediately and then it started. Even though we each had other partners, we were locked in a full-scale competition to out dance one another.

I gave it everything I had, but I was no match for the redhead. My partner finally had enough and said she wanted to sit down. I escorted her to her table, thanked her, and then joined Brian at the bar.

"Did you see that gorgeous redhead out there? She must be a professional dancer."

Just then Lucy reappeared. "Hi guys, I thought you were coming back to the table to join us?"

As we stood there chatting I glanced over Lucy's shoulder and I saw the redhead leaving the dance floor with her partner. She said something to him and he headed in the opposite direction.

Great, I thought; *she is not with him*. Then to my great surprise and delight she walked straight across the dance floor directly toward us, with a big smile on her face and stopped beside Lucy.

Before I could utter a word, Lucy said, "This is my friend Deborah; the one I was telling you about."

It turned out my hunch was correct; Deborah had been a professional dancer. After many years of formal training, her dream of being a ballerina ended in an automobile accident. She had turned to jazz dancing as it was much easier on her injured neck. This, however, did not pay the bills, so she turned to modeling. She had spent the previous two years working as a model in Europe and had returned home to Canada six weeks ago after breaking her leg in Switzerland. She had the cast removed that morning. She and Lucy had been sitting at a table in the back of the club so she could prop her leg up on a chair and diminish the swelling.

I had walked to the gym, so the girls offered to drive me back to my apartment. I didn't want to appear too eager, so I contained my excitement. I got out of the car, thanked them, and walked straight to the door without looking back. Like an idiot, I thought I was being "cool."

As they drove off Deborah stood out of the car sunroof and yelled, "Don't forget to write."

That was it. I was going to get her address from Lucy on Monday and mail her a letter. Canadian mail is notoriously slow, so it took four days before we were on our first date.

"Here, let me get the door for you." I rushed to open the passenger door of my newly purchased Volvo. I was just as surprised as Deborah when a pile of McDonald's food wrappers and boxes fell out of the car onto the pavement. "Sorry! Let me take care of that." I picked up the garbage and threw it into the back seat. "There you go." I motioned for her to get in the car.

"But there is no room for my legs."

"Sure there is. Just squash the wrappers down with your feet."

She reluctantly got in and I closed the door and scooted around to the driver's side.

"I can't believe you have all this McDonalds garbage in your car. The back seat is full of wrappers as well."

"My friends call it the *McVolvo*; I intend to clean it out soon."

And we were off, driving around Stanley Park. Deborah leaned toward me, I thought I was going to get a kiss on the cheek, when she whispered, "I love the smell of deep fry in the evening don't you?"

Convenience was king for me when it came to food. Slow had no meaning in my life. I ate anything that was fast and convenient. My hyperactivity, which had followed me into adulthood, required a lot of fuel, and I was not particularly concerned where it came from. My five-foot-eleven frame carried a solid one hundred and eighty five pounds. I worked out and participated in some sports activity every day; not because I had to, rather because I loved it. Hyperactive children grow into hyperactive adults. It was a curse for my parents and teachers when I was a child but it has served me well my entire adult life when it came to keeping in shape and controlling my Tourette's.

As my relationship with Deborah grew, we would often run, ski, and dance all in the same day. I would gulp down anything that would keep my blood sugar up. We frequently found ourselves in the company of Lucy and her sister Gwen. They were constantly railing on me about my terrible eating habits. They were both proponents of *health food,* whatever that meant.

I became so annoyed at their constant preaching that I once said in anger, "Look at the two of you, and look at me. I think I will stick to my junk food, thanks." Then I ordered a second piece of cheesecake, just to annoy them.

Then the pendulum swung, and oh, did it swing. I caught a cold in mid-January and I could not shake it until well into March. I tried everything, without success. No amount of antibiotic or cold medication had any effect.

Deborah would say, "McDave, time for you to look at what you are eating."

Finally, I read Linus Pauling's book on ascorbic acid (vitamin C), for which he won the Nobel Prize. He clearly states that large doses of vitamin C will help prevent a cold but have little or no effect once the virus has taken hold. Regardless, I started taking six thousand units of vitamin C a day, and within three days the infirmity that had zapped my energy and enthusiasm for the past eight weeks was gone, completely gone.

I am sure it was just a coincidence and I would have had the same recovery without the vitamin C, but it sparked my quest for more knowledge. I started reading everything I could about vitamins and minerals and this quickly spread to nutrition in general; it became my new obsession. I quickly became an encyclopedia of information and misinformation. This is another symptom of TS and OCD: You see we become fixated on things. And even though I was fixated on Deborah; this food thing pulled focus from her and she began to resent it.

"Waiter, would you take this disgusting white bread with no nutrition off the table and bring us some whole grain rolls? You can take the butter too."

"But, David I want some butter, and I love sourdough bread," Deborah pleaded.

"No you don't. You are not eating fat and anything that is bleached, and that flour has been bleached." I stole it out of her mouth. "Most of the calories come from saturated fat. Do you know what that does to your cardiovascular system?"

"David, lighten up. A month ago you started your day with cheesecake to get your sugar levels up because you said all food turns into sugar anyway, and it saved your body all that work. Now, McDave, you're stealing food out of my mouth."

Within a few months I went from a junk food junkie to health food zealot. The nutrition I preached was simple. No white flour, refined sugar, or fat of any kind. I read and understood every label on every package. I memorized tables and tables of food compositions so I had the scientific facts to back up my preaching. When it was my turn to order in a restaurant I would question the poor waiter as to the exact components and method of cooking of every dish I was considering ordering. Frequently they would have to go back into the kitchen to get the answer two or three times before I would place my order. Waiters hated me, chefs hated me, and my friends started to hate me.

Finally my friend Wayne sat me down. "Dave, we need to talk. You are driving everyone away. No one wants to be around you when there is food present. I know you think you are helping but in reality you are driving all your friends away. People feel guilty enough when they are eating; they don't need you preaching at them. Have you noticed that no one wants to go to dinner with you anymore? You have to back off, for your own good."

I still adhere to my nutritional beliefs, but now I give dietary advice only when someone asks for it, and they are usually sorry they did.

My decision on food selection is based solely on nutrition. Taste is not a factor. The taste buds in our mouths only register sweet, sour, salty and bitter. Most of what we call taste is in reality smell.

Thanks to Bobby Garrigan breaking my nose with his thunderous right hook, eighty percent of my sense of smell is gone, along with most of my enjoyment of food. On the bright side, I never crave any food. I have often thought that surgically severing the olfactory nerve or spraying the nasal cavity with a chemical to knock out the sense of smell would be an excellent means of weight control for those who are constantly battling the obesity problem.

"David, my agent says I need to go to Los Angeles if I want this career to go anywhere." said Deborah. "He's right. You have to go where the jobs are. There are few acting opportunities here in Vancouver." " But I don't want to go."

Deborah had the good fortune to land a supporting role in a major motion picture, *Middle Age Crazy*, with Bruce Dern and Ann-Margaret. Ninety-five percent of actresses never get a chance to perform at that level and what is more amazing is that it was her first acting job.

She flew to Toronto to attend the Canadian premier and was escorted to the event by my father, who happened to be visiting the city on business. Afterward she told him she didn't want to leave Vancouver and didn't want to leave me. Bob, the traitor, said, "Deborah, you can always get married, and as much as I would like to see you marry David, you have to pursue this dream. You'll regret it all your life if you don't try."

Four weeks later we packed all we could into Deborah's old Buick convertible and drove the fourteen hundred miles south to LA and the start of her new life. I visited her often. Each time she drove me to the airport I hugged her and walked straight to the plane without looking back.

Years later, she asked me about that. "David, I would be crying, watching you leave, waiting on the last second before the plane left my part of the sky and you never looked back, never waved, and I would feel so cold and hurt."

I never looked back because I had trained myself to sever my emotions. People who have been isolated and rejected for their abnormalities learn to shut down. We become experts. So, I needed to stare straight ahead, to get to that plane, and not let my feelings get in the way. Sometimes my Tourette's conspires to rob me of the ability to sustain a consistent emotional base. It has become my way of life.

"Oh, Dorothy Do You Skate?"

We drove Deborah's beat-up Buick convertible up the long U-shaped drive and parked in front of the beautiful Beverly Hills home. After a quick mirror check of her hair and makeup, we mounted the steps and rang the bell. We were soon greeted by a handsome young man.

"Hi, beautiful; you're late as usual."

Deborah hugged him and said, "This is my boyfriend, David. He was at the show tonight. David, this is Dean."

I had flown into LA earlier that day to see Deborah and her co-star, Dean Martin Jr., perform for the final night of their two-person play at the Hail Theater. This was the post-production party. Deborah knew most of the 16 people milling about inside and introduced me to each one. Although they were all involved in some aspect of show business, the only one I recognized, other than Dean, was his friend, Desi Arnaz, Jr.

A very pretty, athletic-looking blond with short hair introduced herself as Dean's wife, Dorothy, and asked what I would like to drink.

"Do you live in LA, David?" she asked.

"No, I live in Vancouver. I just flew in this morning to see the play and it was a pretty scary flight."

"What kind of plane did you come in on?" asked the male voice behind me.

I spun around and was surprised it was Dean. Before I knew it, a full-blown conversation on aviation erupted. I told Dean the story of my father flying during the war and my upbringing as a hanger rat. His eyes grew wider and his voice quickened the more we talked about airplanes.

"Come with me. I want to show you something you will love."

He led me to his den, which was filled with incredible models of fighter jets. "I'm obsessed with planes. This is my favorite," he said, carefully handing me the model of an F4 Phantom with great pride. "It's the one I fly now."

He went on to explain he was in the Air Force reserve and these were the models of all the fighters he had flown. We talked for a long time, and it was obvious that flying these amazing machines was truly his passion.

"What did you two get lost in?" asked Deborah when we returned to the living room.

"Dean has probably been boring him with all those model planes," said Dorothy.

Nothing could have been further from the truth. I have always been interested in flying and even more interested in hearing people talk about their true passion, regardless of what it is.

The living room seated all sixteen of us comfortably. I was in the middle of one of the couches with Deborah to my left and Dorothy to my right. Suddenly the music changed, and it was an instrumental I did not recognize.

Someone on the other side of the room said, "This must be some of Dorothy's skating music."

I turned to Dorothy, seated beside me, and said, "Oh, Dorothy, do you skate?"

You would have thought I had just expelled the world's longest, loudest, most odoriferous fart. Everyone was staring at me and my face exploded into uncontrollable twitches and grimaces – full blown 'umbrella lady' stuff. I looked at Deborah for some kind of explanation or support. *What had I said wrong?* She rolled her eyes in embarrassment.

Dorothy eventually realized my innocent question was not intended as a joke. She graciously broke the awkward silence. "Yes,

David, I skate."

My parents were surprised I didn't own a TV when they visited me during my sophomore year in college. Two days after they returned home, their gift of a twenty-one-inch RCA television arrived. Three weeks later I sold it for beer money. It was my first and last television. I knew who Dorothy Hamill was, but not having a television, I had no idea what she looked like. How was I to know she was married to Dean Martin Jr.? Once again I heard someone mutter that old familiar whisper, "What's wrong with him?"

Deborah said she loved my energy and that I was different. "He doesn't have his finger on remotes, or the pulse of entertainment, he's too busy doing," she would say. Turns out that Deborah liked my tics, because for her they were a barometer. The more I liked her, the more feelings I had for her, the more my tics would increase. She had her finger on the pulse of my emotions. And, I felt safe, with her.

Several years later I was saddened to learn that Dean's passion had killed him. His F4 Phantom crashed into the side of a California mountain, during a blinding snow storm.

CHAPTER SIXTEEN
"THE APARTMENT BELOW"

My parents came to visit me in Vancouver three or four times a year, and each visit lasted a month or more. They loved the city. My apartment had two bedrooms and two bathrooms, so it was never an inconvenience having them visit, although I did have to put a sign on my bedroom door: *Do not even think about disturbing before 7 am.*

I loved having them there. One day my father said, "Your mother and I have talked it over; you are a single guy with your own life. It's not right for your parents to move in three or four months a year. We have decided to get our own place and we will probably come out even more often."

"That's crazy," I interrupted. "It'll just sit empty half the year and besides, I love it when you visit."

"We've made up our minds; we're going to start looking for our own place tomorrow."

There was no convincing them otherwise. Each evening they would scour the classifieds and make a list of the *apartments for rent* to see the following day. I was always home from work before they returned from their day of apartment hunting. They would drag themselves through the door and flop on the couch.

"Well, how did it go?"

"Not well. We saw eighteen places today, some had nice views but no parking; others had the parking and views but were too far from the downtown. Some had a nice gym and pool but were too far from Stanley Park. I think you have the only place in the city with everything. We'll try again tomorrow."

And try they did. Each day they returned wearier than the day before. Friday, the fifth day was different. I was very surprised when I came home from work and saw them sitting in my living room enjoying a cocktail, at four-thirty in the afternoon.

Without spilling a drop of his scotch, my father jumped to his feet. "We found it! We found it! We're celebrating! It's everything we wanted; fantastic view, great balcony, downtown, and close to Stanley Park. There's underground parking, a gym, an indoor pool, and we don't have to sign a long-term lease."

"Good for you. That sounds perfect; where is it?"

They looked at one another, paused, and then my father said. "Ok, there is one thing that you may not think is perfect. We've rented a nice one bedroom apartment; it's directly four floors below."

It took a minute for this to sink in. "Four floors below, in this building?"

"Yes, but we don't have to sign the agreement until tomorrow so if you don't think it is a good idea we can back out."

I burst out laughing. "Are you kidding? Let's go sign it now."

So the most significant people in my life became my neighbors. It was a phenomenal arrangement. I would frequently lean over the balcony and inquire, "What's for dinner?" I had two cars but my father insisted on buying a used Subaru and left it in the basement when they returned to their home on the east coast. I had many friends who would come and visit for a week or two. If this occurred when my parents were not using their place, my guests had their own apartment and Subaru. Visiting Dave became quite popular.

CHAPTER SEVENTEEN
"A PAIN IN THE NECK"

I was in the Olympic gym doing a seated military press. To perform this exercise correctly, you sit on a bench in front of a rack that holds the barbell at shoulder level behind you. I had reached back, grabbed the weight and pressed it over my head until my arms were locked straight up. The motion puts a tremendous amount of strain on the neck so it is imperative to keep your head straight and look directly forward while performing the exercise.

"HEY!"

I was so startled by the abrupt scream coming from behind that my head reflexively jerked around. The Tourette's may have exacerbated the movement. Pain immediately shot from my neck, to my shoulder, and into my arm. Instantly all strength on the left side of my torso vanished and the heavy barbell I had been pressing over my head tipped to the left and crashed to the floor, taking me with it.

I lay on the floor stunned for a few seconds and then two people—including Bert, the idiot who startled me by yelling—ran to my assistance. They helped me to my feet. The pain was extreme and I was shocked when I saw my reflection in the mirror. My head was bent so far to the left side that my ear was touching my shoulder. I looked like someone hanging from a gallows but without the rope. I reached over with my right arm and tried pulling my head up straight but the shoulder and neck muscles were in such spasm this was impossible. My facial muscles were in full-blown twitch mode but thanks to the muscle spasm my head jerking had stopped completely, at least for the time being. Perhaps there really is a silver lining in every cloud.

I lay back down on the floor while someone ran to get ice. Eventually I got up and although my head was still cocked to the left, it was considerably better than it had been twenty minutes before. I slowly made my way to the dressing room, gathered my things, and without changing, cautiously shuffled to the car and drove myself home.

A sleepless night followed and by the morning the pain had significantly intensified, although I was able to straighten my neck. I knew of an excellent chiropractor not far from my clinic that was open on Saturdays. I called and was told to come in right away. Several radiographs and an examination resulted in a soft tissue injury and muscle spasm diagnosis. Ice, rest, anti-inflammatory and pain medications were prescribed.

The pain worsened Sunday; the relentless toothache-like pain extended through my shoulder and down my left arm. Since I did not normally work Mondays, I went to see my family physician, who immediately sent me to the neurologist. After more x-rays and a cat scan ensued. I was diagnosed with a cervical disc herniation and nerve impingement. More pain medication, muscle relaxants, and traction were prescribed.

I called my receptionist and cancelled the next two weeks at work. Many long, sleepless nights followed. I spent hours sitting in a chair at home with a harness fitted underneath my chin and around the back of my head. Directly above the chair was a pulley attached to the ceiling. One end of a rope was attached to the harness I was wearing and the other went around the pulley and was attached to an iron weight. The traction was supposed to draw the vertebrae apart, align them, relieve the pressure on the disc, and eliminate the pain. It did nothing except make my jaw very sore. Two weeks went by without any relief. My head jerks and twitching worsened.

The pain and chronic lack of sleep were taking a terrible toll. My only relief came from Percocet and Valium, but I hated how they made me feel. I cancelled two more weeks of work.

"Be patient," the neurologist kept saying.

Twenty-nine days later, I called Barry Pass, a neurosurgeon I knew from the hospital and saw him that Friday afternoon. He sent me straight to the hospital and ordered a laminagram, a procedure in which a dye is injected just below the covering of the spinal cord. I was strapped to a table which was quickly turned upside down so the dye would drain toward my head. When the dye reached the level of my neck, a series of quick x-rays were taken and then I was immediately brought to an upright position before the dye reached my brain, which could have disastrous consequences. Afterward I was taken up to the sixth floor where I would have to stay overnight.

"Dr. Bardsley, you are supposed to remain in bed and be as still as possible," said the stout woman in the rose-colored uniform who resembled a fire hydrant more than a nurse, "Otherwise you will become very nauseated,"

"Don't worry about me. I feel perfectly normal."

I felt so good I wandered around the floor, went to the visitors' lounge, and talked to anyone who would listen to me, all the time ignoring repeated instructions to return to my room and lie down. I thought, *That is probably good advice for ordinary patients but I am far more physically fit than most, and I feel terrific.*

I asked for some food but was told I could not eat as it would make me nauseous. I went straight to the vending machine in the visitors' lounge and bought two chocolate bars which I quickly devoured. An hour later, I was sitting beside my bed watching TV when the first tsunami of nausea hit. I bolted to the bathroom but it was too late. I lost all track of time and do not know how long I knelt on the floor, hugging the bowl and retching. Eventually two male orderlies arrived, picked me up by the armpits, and dragged me back to the bed.

I vaguely remember the nurse mumbling something about, "Why don't you listen?" as she jammed a needle into my good shoulder. More waves must have followed because my next recollection was of once again being pried from the toilet bowl I was hugging and dragged back to the bed.

I knew it must be the next day because daylight streamed through the window. My clothes were gone and I was wearing only a surgical gown. My head was swimming. I was very confused. "What's going on?" I protested.

"What do you mean? Dr. Pass explained everything to you yesterday" said the nurse, obviously annoyed.

"What? I haven't seen Dr. Pass!" Before I knew it, there was an IV in my arm and I was in la-la land.

The elevator door closed. "Hey, where are we going?" I slurred.

"To the OR," replied the orderly very matter-of-factly.

"What for?"

"So you can have your surgery."

"What surgery?"

Moments later I was on the OR table, and the anesthetist was leaning over me explaining what was going to happen. Then he attached a syringe to the intravenous line.

"Wait, wait! I need to speak to Dr. Pass first."

"He is outside scrubbing."

"I want to talk to him first."

A few moments later Barry entered the OR with his hands held up in front of him, water running off his elbows. The nurse passed him a sterile towel.

"Barry, whasss going on?" I slurred.

"What do you mean? I explained it all to you last night in your room. I am going to remove the ruptured disc from your neck and do a Cloward procedure to stabilize the vertebrae with a bone graft. Just relax."

Then it was lights out. When I awoke I was back in my room, alone. I immediately noticed the pain in my throat, and a large bulbous bandage protruded from the front of my neck but for the first time since the accident, there was no pain in my shoulder or arm. A few moments later the nurse entered the room.

"Well, Dr. Bardsley. How are you feeling?"

I tried to reply but my throat was on fire.

"Are you going to listen to us today?"

I nodded my head in sheepish compliance.

"Good. Now keep sipping this ice water; it will make your throat feel much better and hydrate you, then we can remove the IV. Do you want something for the pain?"

I motioned I did not. My throat pain improved somewhat over the next hour and several more times the nurse asked if I wanted pain medication. Each time I declined. The absence of pain in my shoulder and arm quickly turned into excitement, then euphoria. It was gone, completely gone. The neck and throat pain were minor in comparison to what I had suffered over the past month. I reached for the phone beside my bed and started calling everyone I knew to tell them the great news. Many I had not spoken to for a long time and they were not even aware I was having any problem. I didn't care; I told them anyway.

Finally, the nurse returned. "I have some morphine for you."

"No. I don't want it!" The orders were PRN. (This is a hospital code which means the medication is only given at the patient's request.)

"I don't care if you are Dr. Bardsley; you are my patient and you are going to get it anyway. You are just too rambunctious for your own good."

Before I could protest, she lifted up the sheet and darted me in the hip with a syringe. Moments later I was totally relaxed with no desire to talk to anyone. It was just what I needed at the time. Unfortunately that kind of nursing rarely exists today.

I was released the next morning wearing a neck brace and given an appointment to see Dr. Pass in his office the following week to have the sutures removed. Recovery was rapid. I called Barry at home to thank him and explained everything was healing well and that I would remove the sutures myself and call him if any difficulties arose.

I returned to work three weeks later. There were still ten weeks left in the ski season. Although Dr. Pass had warned me that a fall would be very dangerous and not to ski until the following year, I could not resist the temptation of my passion. I was on staff at the local veteran's hospital, although I did little surgery there, but they had a prosthesis department where they made a wide variety of artificial limbs. I called the head of the department, Roy Mason, and made an appointment.

"Roy, I am sure you have never been asked to do something like this before, but do you think you could fabricate a brace that will keep my neck from bending even if I crash skiing?"

"Well, Dr. Bardsley, as you know, we specialize in limbs here, but my technicians are very creative. Come with me and let's see what they say."

It took three fittings, but they did it. The base of the brace rested on my shoulders and tapered up to the underside of my jaw and base of my skull. It resembled a Darth Vader helmet with the face missing, but it worked. When I strapped it on, my head simply could not move, in any direction. I had to twist at the waist to see to my side.

I headed to Whistler to join my friends. My intellect told me to heed Dr. Pass's advice, but my Tourette's driven obsession was in control. Passion ruled. Although the facial tics continued, the head jerks were completely absent, as long as I was wearing the brace. There certainly is a silver lining in every cloud.

"*Frozen With Fear*"

> *"276 days to Ru's birthday, please make a note of it,"*
> *"247 days until Ru's birthday, please make a note of it."*

We had been going out for almost a year and each month I would find a new reminder written on my calendar. "Well, what would you like for your birthday Ru?"

"I want us to go sky diving."

"What! Are you crazy? You know heights are the one thing I'm terrified of. Anything, pick anything else."

She held her ground. "Skydiving or nothing."

We arrived at the air strip promptly at eight. We met the instructor, Jim, and the other four people who would be taking the class with us.

Jim explained, "Ground school will last four hours, then you will make two jumps after lunch. This is not tandem jumping. You will exit the plane alone but you will be connected by a fifty-foot static line which will automatically pull the rip cord on your chute, in case you freeze and forget everything."

Over the next four hours we learned how parachutes are made and packed; how to steer and stall them; how to assume the spread-eagle position on exiting the plane; and how to tuck and roll when you hit the ground. I was so nervous about the impending jump I could not eat any lunch.

Jim noticed my facial contortions intensifying and took me aside. "You don't have to jump you know; it's not for everyone."

"I'll be fine…I think."

Finally, it was time. We got into our jump suits, grabbed our parachutes and started walking toward the plane. I was sure I would die of fright before we were ever airborne.

Jim gathered us beside the plane. "Now, the most important thing of all: As you can see, a large section of the side has been removed so we can enter and exit the plane easily. Your emergency chute is spring loaded and its rip cord is located right here on your chest. If it is accidently deployed inside the plane, this is what can happen."

He produced two large photos. The first showed a plane flying with the tail completely tangled in a bright multicolored parachute. The second showed the same plane crashed on the ground with the parachute still wrapped hopelessly around the tail.

"This happened here two years ago. No one was killed, but two were seriously injured. As you can see, there is no door on the side of the plane. When we get in, you will be kneeling, facing forward. Use one hand to hold onto the plane, and the other must be covering the rip cord to prevent accidental deployment of your emergency chute. Do you understand?"

The blood drained from everyone's face. I looked around hoping someone else wanted to back out. I hated Ruanne at that moment.

Jim got in where the passenger's seat would normally have been and knelt, facing the rear. The other five packed in tightly, kneeling and facing forward. I was the last one in. I pushed in tightly against Ru to my left and to my right was the large opening which had been cut in the side of the plane for our easy exit.

As the plane revved up, Jim yelled, "One hand on the plane, one hand covering your rip cord."

We quickly gained speed and moments later we were airborne. The knot in my stomach tightened. Then things got worse, much worse. Within a few minutes of take-off, the plane started to spiral upwards in a clockwise direction. The plane was tilted to the right, so I felt the weight of everyone to my left leaning into me and I was next to the opening. I nearly fell out. I immediately took my protective hand off the emergency rip cord and clamped on to the edge of the opening with both hands.

"Cover your rip cord!" Jim screamed over the roar of the engine.

"I can't, damn it! I'm going to fall out."

The painful cramps in my forearms were almost unbearable by the time the plane stopped spiraling and leveled off. My heart felt like it was going to burst out between my ribs.

Jim grabbed the loose end of the static line and snapped it onto my rip cord "This is it. We are over the jump zone. GO!"

Every part of my body froze except my face and head which were twitching and jerking uncontrollably.

"Stop making those faces. GO!" he yelled.

I looked to my right and saw the three thousand feet of air I would fall through before I would splat on the ground.

"Now!" he screamed.

"I can't."

"You are blocking the exit. If you don't jump no one else can get out, and we'll have to land."

I looked down once more and then suppressed every survival instinct that had been bred into the human body over the past two million years. I plunged headfirst into certain death.

"When you exit, dive into the spread eagle position, arms and legs apart," they tell you in ground school. What they neglect to tell you is that you will immediately be hit by a hundred-mile-an-hour blast of wind from the propeller, which will spin and twist you so that in an instant you lose all sense of orientation. The terror of those first few seconds was so extreme I think I blacked out.

I was jolted back into reality by the jerk of the harness into my groin. Suddenly I realized I was vertical, and my brain started to compute. I immediately looked up to make sure the canopy was fully open and none of the shrouds lines were crossed. I screamed, more from relief than excitement, as I steered the chute towards the landing zone three thousand feet below. The glide was amazingly quiet and lonely.

I hit the ground much harder than we had practiced earlier in the morning. Nonetheless, I was elated it was over. I watched Ruanne float down like a feather and make a perfect bull's eye landing.

Vigorous physical activity had always had a profoundly beneficial effect in lessening the severity of my Tourette and ADHD symptoms. Terror, I learned, had the exact opposite effect. From that day on, Ruanne received a box of chocolates and flowers on her birthday.

"Are You Epileptic?"

"*But if you see me walking by and the tears are in my eyes, look away, baby, look away.*"

The year was 1989, and "Look Away," Chicago's number one hit, was blaring on the car stereo. I slowed my Jeep and rolled to a stop behind a white Chevy van with the words Bosa Mechanical written across the back. The light had just changed to red and I leaned forward to crank up the volume.

BANG.

My head jerked backward with a violent motion until it collided with the headrest, then it ricocheted forward until the seatbelt engaged and abruptly stopped my forward progress. The neck pain was immediate and I was unable to move my head. Glancing in the rearview mirror I saw a huge chrome grill where only moments before the rear window had been. Nothing else was visible.

My first instinct was to open the door and get out of the Jeep. *Oh. God! My neck fusion has broken loose*, was my next thought. I did not try to open the door or roll down the window. I sat immobile and a few moments later someone appeared beside the door.

"Are you OK?"

"No, I have a problem with my neck."

"Just stay there. I am calling for help right now."

Within minutes the ambulance arrived. They tried to open the driver's door but it was welded shut by the impact. "Are you hurt?" the ambulance attendant yelled through the glass.

"I have a cervical fusion; I think it has broken loose."

"Don't move. The fire department is on its way. Are you an epileptic? Have you ever had a seizure?"

"No."

I thought it a very strange question considering the circumstances. It took them only minutes to remove the door with the Jaws of Life. The attendant carefully fitted me with a cervical collar while I remained seated. The firemen then used the Jaws of Life to remove the jammed back hatch and the passenger seat.

I overheard the ambulance attendant say to one of the firemen, "I think he is having some kind of seizure." It took a few seconds for his words to sink in. The stress of the accident must have exacerbated my Tourette symptoms, which they mistook for a seizure.

"I am not having a seizure," I blurted, "I have Tourette Syndrome."

A stretcher was quickly slid into place and I was carefully manipulated onto it and strapped down, all the while maintaining traction on my neck. "I can feel and move my arms and legs," I kept repeating, "but there is something digging into my back."

"Don't worry about that now; we will take care of it when we arrive at the hospital."

After a quick assessment was made in the emergency department, I was whisked off to radiology. Despite my complaints, little attention was given to the pain in my back and shoulder area and I remained firmly strapped to the backboard for forty five minutes while the radiographs were taken and developed. Finally, the diagnosis came.

"The good news is that your cervical fusion is intact but you have sustained considerable soft tissue damage to your neck." exclaimed the ER doctor.

"What exactly does that mean?"

"You have a severe acceleration – deceleration injury—a whiplash."

I was finally unstrapped from the backboard and allowed to sit up. "Oh my God!" exclaimed the nurse. "You have a dozen chards of glass stuck in your back. Why didn't you say something?"

I just rolled my eyes. Following their removal, I was discharged with anti-inflammatory and narcotic pain medications and told to contact my family physician in three or four days.

As far as I was concerned, whiplash was an imaginary disorder claimed by malingerers trying to extract money from insurance companies. I was ashamed to tell anyone I had whiplash. I called the clinic and told them I would be back to work in three days.

Things got worse, much worse, and for a very long time. As long as I kept my head upright on the vertical plane, the pain was minimal. When I bent forward or flexed my neck in any direction, the pain quickly became intolerable. When I returned to work I was able to do consultations and short examinations without much difficulty but flexing forward to perform surgery was excruciating.

Over the course of the next twelve months, a total of two hundred and sixty different treatments were performed on my neck and shoulder areas. Muscle relaxants, pain killers, chiropractic manipulations, massage therapy, Rolfing, chelating therapy, traction, transcutaneous nerve stimulation, acupuncture, nerve blocks— nothing seemed to help. The more surgery I performed, the worse it became. The pain was becoming intolerable. It was having serious effects on my work, my relationships, and my moods. There seemed to be no end to the suffering. Things couldn't get any worse.

CHAPTER EIGHTEEN
"THE CIRCLE OF LIFE"

"Clear."

Thud . *Beep, beep, beep, beeeeeeeeeeeeeeeeep.*

Flatline. *God, please no, please.* "Three hundred watts," I barked.

"*Oui*, Doctor."

"Clear."

Thud. *Beep, beep, beep.*

"Adrenaline, more adrenaline."

"*Oui*, Doctor. Atropine?"

"Yes, atropine. Three, *trois* milligrams."

Beep, beep, beep.

It quickly became the sweetest most beautiful sound I had ever heard, the sound of life itself. Then just as suddenly, it was snatched away, replaced by the squeal of death. *Beeeeeeeeeep.*

I pointed to his nose, and the nurse quickly applied the mask and started squeezing the life-sustaining oxygen into his lungs. I pounded my fist at the base of his sternum and followed with progressively harder thrusts with both palms to the chest wall directly over his stalled heart

"Six, seven, eight." I could hear the ribs cracking with each compression. I frantically grabbed the paddles again.

"Maximum, four hundred watts. Clear."

Thud.

Nothing, just the horrifying squeal: *Beeeeeeep.*

"Bicarbonate."

"*Oui*, Doctor."

"Clear."

Thud.

His lifeless body was jolted three or four inches off the table. The skin surrounding the dish-shaped deformity on his chest wall was burnt bright red. The sound of death shrieked…

Beeeeeeep.

I started the compressions again, "More adrenaline."

"*Oui*, Doctor."

"Seven, eight, nine. Clear."

Thud. *Beep, beep, beep, beep.*

"Thank you, God. Thank you."

The surreal battle of life and death oscillated back and forth. Twenty-five minutes later it ended, when the nurse put one hand on my shoulder, pointed to his head and then the clock. Without speaking a word, her message was crystal clear. Even if I could start his heart one more time, the brain damage would be insurmountable.

It was not until that moment that I snapped out of my doctor mode and the full gravity of the situation hit me. For the first time in my life, I was numb, completely numb. Disbelief eventually gave way to reality. There, on the table, lay my teacher, my mentor, my biggest supporter, and the best friend I ever had—my father, Bob.

Throughout all my difficult early years, he was always there, providing unyielding support, relentless encouragement, and uncompromising love. Now, when he needed me most, I failed him.

Where would I ever find the courage to explain to my mother, waiting in the adjacent room, what had just happened?

I didn't have to.

When I turned toward the exit, there she was, standing in the half-open doorway. She had witnessed everything. Moments later, the tears gushed as we stood hugging each other beside his lifeless body. The nurses quietly slipped out.

"Dave, I want to be alone with your father for a few minutes."

I stepped outside and waited.

Just thirty minutes before, I could hardly contain my excitement. I was at Charles de Gaulle airport in Paris, standing ten feet in front of the doors to the Jetway at gate 72. I knew my parents would be so surprised to see me. We had arranged to meet outside of customs and immigration with all the other passengers. I wanted to surprise them, so I had gone to customs earlier and explained that I was a doctor and that my father was arriving shortly from Canada and that he was very sick and would need my help. Little did I know that cruel fate would turn my lie into reality. Security in 1990 was nothing compared to what it is today. They believed my story and let me through. I had not seen my parents for four months.

The doors to the Jetway burst open as an Air France employee hurriedly pushed a wheelchair with my father slumped in it. My mother was half a step behind. His color was terrible and he was struggling to breathe. As I rushed toward him I saw panic and terror in his eyes, like a man drowning. He reached out, clutched my arm tightly and strained to communicate.

The attendant explained in broken English that there was a medical clinic in the basement of the airport, two floors below. His distress level quickly escalated as we rushed toward the elevator. My mother explained that everything had been perfect during the flight but as the plane started to descend, Bob starting gasping for air. My mind was racing. I asked if he had been eating, thinking of a food obstruction. He had not.

We arrived at the clinic and went straight into a clean, well equipped treatment room. I asked the Air France attendant to take my mother into the adjacent office and to please stay with her. I lifted my father onto the bed with the help of two nurses, neither of whom spoke English. One quickly fitted an oxygen mask and his color improved slightly. I saw an EKG machine in the corner and pointed to it. She said something in French and instantly started connecting the leads to his chest.

My father's color continued to improve and his anxiety level decreased somewhat. His pulse was slow and his blood pressure a little below normal; otherwise things were stable. I grabbed a stethoscope and listened to his lungs; they seemed to be full of fluid. The rhythmic beeping of the EKG monitor was a wonderfully reassuring sound.

My father reached up and grabbed my right arm and tried to speak; he was terrified. I looked at him through the transparent oxygen mask and smiled. "Everything is going to be all right," I said.

The words had barely crossed my lips when I saw his eyes roll back and then I heard that unforgettable squeal: *Beeeeeeep.*

Flat line.

"Please God, no."

Everyone was extremely kind and respectful despite our limited ability to communicate. I guess the pain of grief is the same regardless of language and culture. I left my mother alone in the room with her husband and soul-mate of forty-five years. Not knowing where to turn, I called the Canadian embassy for help. Being a weekend, it was closed, but there was an emergency number on the recording, so I called it.

"I am so sorry for your loss," the young attaché said. "I am afraid it's going to take seven or eight days for the body to be properly prepared so it can re-enter Canada. Do not hesitate to call me if I can be of any further assistance."

I called my brothers in Canada and could barely believe my own words as I related the events.

"I'm coming over right now," said Peter, the younger of my two brothers.

"No, not yet Pete. I have no idea what will happen next. I'll call you as soon as I find out."

Much confusion followed. Several gendarmes arrived along with airport security. After much discussion, all in French, an undertaker arrived and my father's body was placed in the hearse and we followed in a police car to a small village ten miles from the airport. It took three or four hours with a pocket dictionary to understand what would happen next. I selected a coffin and the undertaker confirmed it would be seven or eight days before the body would be ready to transport back to Canada. I offered him a large sum of money if he could do it faster.

"*Cinq* days," he said, holding up five fingers.

I nodded my agreement and signed the contract.

"Let's take a cab back to the airport and get on the next flight back to Canada. I will make arrangements with the airline to ship the body as soon as it is ready."

"No," said my mother, defiantly. "I am not leaving here without your father."

No matter how hard I tried to persuade her otherwise, she was not going to leave France without her husband.

"It's going to be five days. What are we going to do here for five days?"

"Your father came here to see the boat; it is all he talked about for months. He would want us to see it, so let's go."

Ever since those days in Colonel Holder's boatyard I had dreamed of sailing into paradise. The previous year I had come to France and visited all the boat manufacturers who built large catamarans. The French were the best in the world at building and sailing catamarans. I finally decided on a forty-five-foot model built in La Rochelle, about an eight-hour drive west of Paris. I had signed the contract and sent the money. The vessel was now ready to be placed on the deck of a freighter and sent the ten thousand miles to Vancouver. The purpose of this trip was to make sure all the modifications had been made and were to my satisfaction because once it landed in Vancouver, I owned it regardless.

My parents loved sailing. My father and I talked for endless hours about sailing into paradise: where we would go, in what order we would visit the different countries, what were the safest routes. He was more excited than me about coming to France and seeing it.

We returned to the airport by cab and I rented a tiny Peugeot, barely large enough to accommodate two adults and three suitcases. We started driving west but within an hour we stopped and found a place to sleep. We had both been awake for more than twenty-four hours.

I called my brothers and told them our plan. To this day I remember absolutely nothing of the next five days. Two weeks after returning to Canada, I received a condolence card from the sales manager of the boat company in La Rochelle. Had it not been for that card I would have sworn we never reached the coast or saw the boat.

I spent hours on the phone making all the arrangements for our return flight and for shipping the body back with Air Canada. It took many calls but everyone I spoke with was reasonably fluent in English. My brothers and Tim Fitzgerald, the funeral director who was my father's very good friend, would meet us on the other end. Fortunately, we arrived at Charles de Gaulle airport three hours before our evening flight was to depart. The lines were huge but we endured.

"Enjoy your flight home," the cheery employee said as she handed us our boarding passes.

Just as we stepped away from the counter, my mother said, "Wait, I want to know for sure that your father is on this plane."

"He is. I have arranged the whole thing. I assure you he is. Please, let's go."

"Ask them to check. I want to make sure."

The attendant overheard some of our conversation and said, "Do you want me to check and see if the passenger you are inquiring about has already checked in?"

I explained the situation and she responded. "I am so sorry. I will call the supervisor and he can check the cargo manifest for you."

We stepped aside and a few minutes later the supervisor appeared and was most helpful. He spent several minutes peering through the tiny glasses perched on the end of his long thin French nose. "I am very sorry, Monsieur, but there are no remains on this flight. They will probably be on the morning flight."

"Come on, Irene. If we don't hurry, we'll miss the plane. He'll be on the next flight."

"I am not leaving France without my husband."

I went to the nearest pay phone and called the number I had been given for Air Canada cargo. An hour later, I hung up in total disbelief. They had no record of receiving my father's body. I looked at my watch. It was forty-five minutes to take-off.

I searched frantically for the number of the funeral parlor and woke the proprietor from a deep sleep. He assured me the body was properly prepared and he had turned it over yesterday to the trucking company for delivery to Air Canada cargo. I could feel the anxiety flood through my body as I waited while he went to look for the phone number of the trucking company. They answered on the tenth ring. Their English was practically nonexistent. It took another hour using the pocket dictionary to explain the reason for my call. Eventually, they found the order to pick up Bob's body at the funeral home and deliver it to air cargo. What they were unable to do was verify that it had been done.

I called air cargo again with the name of the transport company, hoping this might help locate my father's body but still nothing. Now in panic mode I called the undertaker again and he insisted they had picked up the body yesterday. I glanced at my watch; our flight had departed.

My mother and I found an unoccupied alcove in the ticketing area and cried until our eyes were dry. A hopeless, empty, lonely feeling welled up inside of me.

"Oh Dave!" my mother sobbed. "What do we do now?"

"The police. Let's go to the police."

We found a police officer outside the terminal and tried to explain what was happening. I am sure he had no understanding of what I was saying but the urgency and anxiety in my voice was obvious. He called for a car and we were taken to a police station in the same little town as the funeral parlor. What unfolded next was like a scene straight out of *Saturday Night Live* or *Monty Python*.

It was midnight when we arrived at the station. The gendarme behind the front desk cut me off after I had spoken only a few words and led us into an inner office where a balding middle-aged man, two sizes too big for his disheveled uniform, nodded and smiled but said nothing. His name tag read "Pierre LeBlanc, sergeant."

"My father died at the airport and now his body has been lost," I explained, speaking slowly.

The officer kept nodding and smiling. It was obvious he did not understand a single word. I took out my pocket dictionary and tried to piece together a sentence. "*Mon pere a ete tue a l'aeroport, et son corps est absent.*" My father died in the airport but his body is missing.

Sergeant LeBlanc jumped to his feet, rushed out of the office, and said something to the gendarme at the front reception and returned with a form which he placed in front of me, then gave me a pen. It was all in French so I turned to my tiny dictionary and laboriously tried to translate it. The first page was biographical data: the deceased's name, address, age, etc. Sprawled across the top of the second page were the words *Rapport d'Homicide*.

"No, no, not murdered, died at airport, five days ago, body has been lost, my father's body lost, *comprendre*? Lost, body, lost, missing." I repeated.

Finally the expression on his face changed. "*Oui, oui.*" Once again he rushed out to the reception and spoke even faster to the second gendarme. Moments later, he slid another form in front of me, all in French.

"English. Can we find anyone who speaks English?" I pleaded.

"English, no," he shook his head. "Français."

I started translating from the dictionary again. "*Rapport de Personne Absent,*" (Missing Person report).

My frustration level was off the charts; I stood up and started yelling. "He is not missing. He is dead. Dead! Do you understand? His body is missing."

My mother, who had been seated beside me throughout this whole ordeal, grabbed my arm and pulled me back into the chair. She started rubbing my neck and then without saying a word we burst into tears, then laughter, then tears, back to laughter. We oscillated between the two for a good five minutes.

The officer in the reception heard the commotion and came running in. He and Sergeant LeBlanc just stared at us like we had lost our minds. For those five minutes, we had.

"I guess this is payback time. I bet your father regrets making those French jokes now. They are having the last laugh."

The situation was so painful, so frustrating, and so absurd; laughter was the only emotion we had not experienced over the past five days and no matter how inappropriate, it just came out. It was exactly what we needed at the time.

Hours later, at six a.m., an officer arrived for duty who spoke enough English that I could relate what had happened. His father had recently passed away and he was most kind and sympathetic. Many more forms followed and when we had concluded, he gave me the phone number at the precinct and his home phone number and said they would start an investigation right away.

I phoned for an update three times a day for the next four days and finally on the fifth day, Bob's body mysteriously showed up at Air Canada cargo. No one could tell us how long it had been there or who had delivered it. This time, when we checked in for our flight, the Air Canada supervisor was able to assure my mother that her husband was indeed on the same plane.

When we finally arrived at the small airport in Saint John, it was dark. There was no Jetway. As we descended the stairs onto the tarmac, I saw the hearse round the corner of the terminal and stop near the tail of the plane. The dozen people waiting inside strained to see through the dirty windows and darkness. No one truly believed he was gone, until they saw the coffin being unloaded from the plane and placed in the waiting hearse.

My father's family had come to Canada from Bristol, England, one hundred and fifty years before but somehow Bob always considered himself Irish. He always said he wanted an Irish wake; he was finally about to get his wish.

Three days later I was sitting with my family in the front row of the packed church, listening to Father Brian's kind words. People with TS learn early on to isolate their emotions; it is a coping mechanism. I wanted with all my heart and soul to be delivering my father's eulogy but I knew it could never be. I could not isolate myself from the unbearable pain and I knew I would break down, the moment I started to speak.

My brother Peter arranged an incredible Irish wake. That night the band played into the wee hours. Songs were sung, stories told, drinks consumed—just the way Bob would want it. There were prolonged hugs and embraces but most of all there were the tears; necessary, painful, cleansing, healing, celebrating tears.

CHAPTER NINETEEN
"THANKS FOR ASKING"

Several weeks after I had set up my surgery practice in Vancouver, the phone rang one morning and it was my father.

"Hi Dad, how are you? What's going on?"

"Dave, I was wondering, do you have your business cards printed yet?

"I do. Actually I think they just came in last week. Why?

"I was wondering if you would send me some, I would like a hundred."

"What! A hundred? Are you sure?'

"Yep, a hundred please."

"Well OK, if that's what you want."

As I hung up the phone I thought, *How proud my parents must be at the way things have turned out, that my father wants one hundred of my business cards to hand out to his friends and acquaintances*, and a wonderful warm feeling welled up inside me.

It was not until five years after my father's death that I learned the fate of those 100 business cards. Several months before my father was forced to close the old family business he purchased a small insurance agency which included the two story house that contained it. The agency occupied the second floor and there were two rental offices on the ground floor, one on each side. Not long after he purchased the property my father recognized the name on one of those office doors. It was the same child psychiatrist who had diagnosed me as mentally retarded, twenty-one years before.

For 100 days my father barged into the psychiatrist's office, planted himself in front of the desk, reached into his pocket, and took out one of my business cards. Holding it up in front of the psychiatrist he said, "By the way, my son, the RETARDED maxillofacial surgeon, is doing *juuust* fine. Thanks for asking," He slid it across the desk, turned and sauntered out.

EPILOGUE

Throughout my life, and especially during those difficult early years, my parents would say to me over and over, *"You are David Bardsley. You can be anything you want, anything. Never be afraid to try."*

When I tried and failed they would simply say, *"Don't give up, we believe in you; we believe in you; we believe in you."*

After you hear those words a thousand times, something magical begins to happen. The words transform and become. *"I believe in me; I believe in me; I believe in me."*

My father taught by example, not words. He tried and fell short often. He purchased a three unit apartment house but it burned down; the insurance did not cover the mortgage. While running the family business on a full-time basis, he opened a hardware store which failed within two years. He purchased two small apartment buildings which he was eventually forced to sell at a loss. Still, he kept trying and taught me to do the same. He cared little about what others thought of him. He was a tower of strength in his own life and in mine, and now he was gone.

Teddy Roosevelt must have been thinking of my father when he spoke these words:

It is not the critic who counts; not the man who points out how the strong man stumbles, or where the doer of deeds could have done them better. All credit belongs to the man who is actually in the arena, whose face is marred by dust and sweat and blood; who strives valiantly; who errs and comes short again and again; who at the best, knows in the end the triumph of high achievement and who at the worst, if he fails, at least he fails while daring greatly. So that his place shall never be with those timid souls who know neither victory nor defeat.

The apple does not fall far from the tree. There were changes to be made and dreams to be lived. What was I waiting for? The new arena waited. I had spent my entire life knowing I was different. People expected it. Why disappoint them now? For decades psychological studies have confirmed that change is perhaps the one thing people fear the most and will do almost anything to avoid it. My father embraced change and taught me to do the same.

May 29, 1991, my new life began. In the thirteen months after my father's death, I had sold my surgery clinic, my condo, cars, furniture, clothes—everything. What I could not sell, I simply gave away. I would devote my life to fulfilling my two greatest passions; sailing and skiing. I moved what essentials I needed aboard my catamaran and did what I had always dreamed about; I sailed into paradise.

For the next nine years the *MADHATTER* was my home. I was always accompanied by family and friends; sometimes only two, other times eight. She was no *Marina Queen*. We would sail from country to country for eight months; then find a safe port to leave her. Each winter I would return to Colorado, rent a small apartment, and ski every day for four months.

In the spring I returned to the boat, assembled a crew, and sailed for another eight to eighteen months. I frequently picked up friends in one country and dropped them off in another. For the crew it was usually necessary to have a month or more of vacation time, to make the logistics work. As the years passed and my friends married and had children it became increasing difficult to assemble a crew.

In May of 1999 the *MADHATTER* returned to Fort Lauderdale, Florida, following a three week trip to the Bahamas. My friends Bill and Chris flew back to Canada and I awaited the arrival of the next crew, my good friend Doby and his girlfriend Susan. Doby had immigrated to the United States from Germany after college and was living in Tampa. We had met years ago skiing in Aspen. He had arranged a four-week vacation from his gastroenterology practice and the three of us were going to sail to Venezuela, where the *MADHATTER* would spend the next four months, safe from the Atlantic hurricanes.

They had planned to arrive on Tuesday and we would set sail Friday morning. I called his home on Wednesday morning but there was no answer. I called his pager and the answering service said he was away for a month. I busied myself making the boat ready and laying in all the provisions. I tried numerous times on Friday; still no answer.

What on earth could be keeping them? I pondered over and over.

Finally, on Saturday morning, someone picked up his phone. I knew by the thick German accent it was Doby's father. He lived in Germany but I had met him once before.

"Oh, David, terbull asident, terbull; Dobromire deed."

"I'm sorry, I don't understand. Dobromire did what?"

"Deed, asident, car, Dobromire no more, Dobromire deed." Then he burst into tears.

The crushing reality struck me. For the second time in my life, I was totally numb, unable to speak.

Five days before, at three in the morning, Susan and Doby loaded their mountain bikes on top of his car and headed towards the hills of Georgia, for a day of fun. Two hours into the trip they drove into a rain squall. The car hydroplaned, spun into the guard rail and then bounced across two lanes, into the path of an oncoming semi. They died instantly.

As I sat listening to Doby's eulogy, I realized everything eventually comes to an end. It was time for change. Following the service I returned to the marina and put the *MADHATTER* up for sale.

I continued to return to Colorado each winter. I loved being a ski bum. After the boat was sold, I started my adventuring by motorcycle, crisscrossing the United States six times and riding through Europe. My passion for motorcycles then led me to Australia and New Zealand for seven consecutive years, each trip lasting a minimum of three months.

In 2006 my lifelong friend, Ian, retired and bought a waterfront condo on the Caribbean island of Antigua. He bought a smaller version of the *MADHATTER* and proudly docked it in front. We spent many months leisurely sailing from island to island, all the while planning our next big motorcycle adventure.

On June 1, 2008, seven months and two days after we started, we returned to Colorado, following a 36,400 mile ride to the tip of South America and back. We were lucky. There had been many near misses. We often spoke candidly of the danger.

Ian would say, "Better to end my life on the grill of a truck than to languish in a hospital bed with some terminal illness."

We headed back to Canada to visit our families and plan our next ride. It would be to the Arctic Circle. This adventure, however, was never to happen.

On a beautiful morning in early July, while returning from a visit with his mother, a truck run a stop sign and broadside Ian's motorcycle, killing him instantly.

It has been eighteen years now since I stopped practicing surgery. I have spent the entire time pursuing my passions and fulfilling my dreams. Perhaps now it is time to start giving back.

I had no burning desire or need write this book or tell my story. I did it hoping that somewhere, somehow, it might help someone. Possibly some other "less than perfect" person, or parent of a "less than perfect" child will read this and understand.

The years have taught me that there is nothing wrong with *being different* but for a child it can be devastating. My parents wisely understood that medication is seldom the answer. Support, encouragement, and love can overcome almost any obstacle or limitation. Give it and receive it freely and without hesitation.

In the end, it's all we really have.

ACKNOWLEDGEMENTS

I would like to thank the following people for their generous commitment of time, effort and encouragement in helping me bring this project to fruition. Lee Pardee, Debra Falender, Clara Khoury, Mary Kennedy Bardsley, Kimberly Hunter, Deborah Wakeham and Kathleen Tracy.